SURVIVING
TOUGH TIMES

· · · · · · · · · · · ·

TWELVE KEYS TO
PULLING THROUGH HARDSHIP

DAVID KATEEBA

HigherLife Publishing and Marketing
PO Box 623307
Oviedo, FL 32762
All rights reserved.

ISBN: 978-1-951492-12-0 Paperback
ISBN: 978-1-951492-13-7 eBook

The words him, his, he, or man are invariably used in a generic sense and in such instances may have reference to people of either gender.

Take note that the name satan and related names are invariably not capitalized. This deliberate dishonor is a choice on the part of the author, despite it being a violation of grammatical rules.

*To my grandson Zaine, whose life from day one has
truly epitomized surviving tough times*

TABLE OF CONTENTS

Acknowledgments 1

Introduction 3

Chapter 1 **Relentless Prayer** 7

Chapter 2 **Reciprocal Promising** 21

Chapter 3 **Reassuring Profession** 51

Chapter 4 **Right Positioning** 71

Chapter 5 **Remaining in Place** 75

Chapter 6 **Resetting Priorities** 83

Chapter 7 **Rising Patiently** 91

Chapter 8 **Rightful Partnership** 99

Chapter 9 **Resolute Purpose** 107

Chapter 10 **Resounding Praise** 113

Chapter 11 **Raw Passion**. 123

Chapter 12 **Regimented Planting** 141

Epilogue 159

ACKNOWLEDGMENTS

I am fully persuaded that the "big guy upstairs" has had the biggest hand in this work's coming to fruition. I am eternally indebted to Him for all I've learned about surviving tough times and now attempt to pass it on to the reader in the pages that follow. Thank You, Lord.

In truth I profess that the best in us always emerges when we identify and collaborate with others who have an eye for the positives in our negatives, the roses amid our thorns, the honey made by our stinging bees, the grapes beneath those towering giants, and the silver lining in the dark clouds within us—others who can spot the crown camouflaged by our cross and the success hidden in our sacrifice. To that end I take pleasure in acknowledging the following people, whose gracious input spurred me on until this book was out:

Pastor Moses N. Sekatawa at Christ Reigns Worship Center in Beltsville, Maryland, for the essential tips you could have very easily kept to yourself. Bless you, sir.

Pastor Joybel K. Tampa at International Gospel Church in Chelsea, Massachusetts, for constantly whooping, "Yes, you can!" and nagging me out of my comfort zone. Just look at the payoff it's brought forth! More grace to you, ma'am.

My wife, Nicola, for being the greatest cheerleader I could have ever asked for. Your timing was always impeccable in providing the lift I needed to get airborne and dotting my i's and crossing my t's when my mid-flight writing vertigo caught up with me, tempting me to retreat.

Linda Muwonge at Destiny Christian Ministries, London, for the critical and incredible logistical support that only you could provide.

The staff, volunteers, and members of the Destiny family, at Destiny Christian Ministries in Battersea, London, for being the calm guinea pigs by which I tested much of what I now share. Thank you for allowing me to experiment on you. You make the mind-boggling job that is pastoring such a blast!

INTRODUCTION

There are situations in life that bring folks to their knees, that drive them to desperation, and from which there seems to be no escape. Even the most hardened macho hustler is stretched to the brink of his tethers in these, as these situations are no respecters of persons. They befall the innocent, the guilty, the saint, the sinner, the good, the bad, the ugly, the bold, the beautiful, the rich, the famous, and everyone in between. Living can be difficult.

As one famous singer sang: "If it ain't one thing . . . it's another." Renowned motivational speaker Les Brown rightly said, "We are in an era that the late Peter Drucker [a former world-renowned, Austrian-born American management consultant, educator, and author] calls the three C's: accelerated change, overwhelming complexity, and tremendous competition."[1]

Those who look cool, calm, and collected have simply mastered the art of depriving their troubles of the oxygen of publicity. Make no mistake, beneath that veneer lurks the raw deal.

We share our world with mathematicians and physicists who believe Murphy's Law, which says, "Anything that can go wrong will go wrong." Life is marbled with deadly situations that seem to defy every conceivable remedy man can humanly doctor. You don't have to go far to see this. The headlines in our tabloids and the breaking news in the media ably, avidly, and regularly treat us to an elaborate menu of trouble in high definition. These situations are not occasional; they're an onslaught, a daily assault.

Jesus, the master miracle worker, told His disciples they would have tribulation in this world. Fortunately, He was quick to add that they were to be of good cheer because He had an excellent track record of dealing with that tribulation. So there is hope.

That hope to make *surviving tough times* a real-life achievement is the theme of this book. Hopefully, this work will dispel and expose the defeatist myth, which insinuates that "what will be, will be"—that we can't make it through the tragedies appointed to snuff us out.

If that myth were true, we would not do a lot of things: We would not wear glasses anymore when we can't see well. Why bother? What will be, will be. We would stop wearing seat belts too and no longer engage the expertise of a mechanic when something breaks down. Why should we? What will be, will be. We would stop visiting dentists and doctors too when we felt sick, and perhaps not even open an umbrella if we are caught in a downpour. Why? Because what will be, will be.

Obviously, soldiering on with life like that is not an option. When our lives are besieged by trouble, we must commit and apply ourselves to corrective measures and actions; we must constantly be focused on improvement and excellence in our lives, especially when problems arise.

If our efforts in this *always* paid off, that would be very encouraging. However, that hardly ever happens, so it is our duty to strive for our own deliverance.

If, for example, we abuse our bodies with irregular sleep patterns, overeating or eating too much processed food, overwork, or the lack of exercise, we cannot blame fate for our troubles. We cannot naively say, "This was bound to happen." No; we had a hand in it.

To the degree that we are able, we must actively prevent bad results stemming from our own choices. We cannot afford to be docile spectators, sloppily dawdling along without engaging in mending our mistakes, and being responsible for our wrongdoing. In truth, none of us will escape the consequences of our actions. None of us gets special seating in the auditorium of our lives.

If the devil is going to bog us down in any way, shape, or form, he is going to have to earn that without our help. We do not want to hand him a landslide victory and make his diabolical agenda easy due to our own laziness. A Chinese proverb says, "Failure is not falling down but refusing to get up."

We must *not* throw in the towel and quit. We also must not rest on the laurels of our past successes. If plan A flops, the alphabet has 25 more letters!

We must be teachable and open to learning new things on one hand and going about old things in a new way on the other. When we are affected by adversity, we must be upbeat about bettering ourselves and helping others. We must not be stopped by stormy seas or handicapped by daunting circumstances. Instead we must learn. Those who fail to learn lessons from the past demonstrate a determination to repeat those mistakes. William E. Gladstone, a former British prime minister, once said, "No man ever became great or good except through many and great mistakes."

In the pages that follow, you will find tried, tested, and true answers to help you deal with trials. Embellished with real-life examples and reinforced with heartwarming tales, as well as scores of biblical principles and concepts that explain the whys and hows behind it all, these stories are from those who have successfully navigated trials. Welcome to the world of survivors. Take your place, fasten your seat belt, and survive!

CHAPTER 1

RELENTLESS PRAYER

*So when he had arrested him, he put him in prison, and delivered him to four squads of soldiers to keep him, intending to bring him before the people after Passover. Peter was therefore kept in prison, but **constant prayer was offered to God** for him by the church.*

—Acts 12:4–5, emphasis added

Unapologetically, I begin with prayer. And no, I'm not some kind of prayer expert. In fact, I am a desperate amateur in this most potent, timeless, noble, and expedient discipline. Interestingly, prayer is perhaps the most difficult, challenging, debated, opposed, and resisted activity we participate in—and that's in the church! It's much worse in nonreligious circles. Viewpoints on prayer are often two-sided and rarely agree.

In one camp, there are avid proponents who make no bones about prayer being the master key that unlocks each and every breakthrough we seek to secure. Real-life testimonies undergird this stance, and with an agelong tradition lending credence to their assertion, these folks rest assured that their beliefs are written in stone and unquestionable.

Camp two carries its own plethora of scriptural references and contends with equal passion a stand completely opposite camp one's. The ideas of those in that camp are also plausible.

The result? There's an incredible array of books on prayer. Authors are keen to write about the middle ground, seeking to present a balanced position on the subject in the hope that their work will help resolve the many questions between the two camps. Bookstores and the internet are awash with new titles on prayer — many screaming, "Me too!" So coming up with a new treatise on the subject is akin to preaching to the choir.

Still, I believe satan and his hordes of helpers in spiritual darkness are greatly hampered in their diabolical agenda when people get down to serious praying. The enemy will do anything to curtail the prayers of God's people even in the smallest way. This only underscores the need for even deeper and more protracted praying.

The devil would sooner tolerate people giving God the highest praises for hours, attending multiple church services, listening to lots of motivational sermons, giving large donations, or running awe-inspiring church programs than have them praying relentlessly to release spiritual resources "on earth as it is in heaven" (Matt. 6:10).

E. M. Bounds candidly noted that:

The Devil often tries to break the soul down and reduce it to despair. In order to discourage us, he tells us that we will never succeed, that the way is too hard and the burden too heavy. He takes advantage of weak, distracted nerves and suggests fears. Grace is hidden from sight, shortcomings are magnified, and weaknesses are classed as gross sins. . . . He darkens the future. Heaven and God are hidden by a thick veil of tomorrow's cares, trials, and needs. The imaginary disasters, failures, and evils of the future are powerful weapons in Satan's hand. He suggests that the Lord is a hard master and that His promises will fail. He works on the corruption that remains in the heart and raises a great storm in the soul.[1]

This is not hard to understand. Prayer is the most powerful discipline available to mankind. A dear old friend of mine, the Reverend Douglas Lott II, often said, "If you won't pray, you won't stay. If you won't fast, you sure won't last."

Prayerlessness is synonymous with powerlessness. Living is not just *hard* without power; it's *impossible*. So is being a witness for Christ. The disciples of the early church were sternly instructed to wait in Jerusalem until they were endowed with power. (See Acts 1:4, 8.) God actually built His forgiveness, healing, and revival on prayer. (See 2 Chron. 7:14.)

A highly acclaimed psychologist is quoted as once having said: "Prayer is the greatest power available to the individual in solving his personal problems. Its power astonishes me."[2]

Rather than teasing and laughing mankind to scorn, the sorrows and hardships we encounter in life are inadvertently saying, "Can't you see that this situation requires something beyond you—

possibly something *divine*—to get you out of the mess you are in?" These situations actually drive us to prayer. They urge us to offer up constant unrelenting prayer long enough to see change manifest.

This is not to suggest we do not take faith-filled action. Instead, that action should be taken against a backdrop of constant, unrelenting prayer.

Prayer is a powerful key to releasing us from whatever restricts, constricts, or traps us or others in awful and unacceptable positions in life. This key is placed in the hands of anyone who will take a stand. Regardless of the pain and oppression, we can pray our way out of these limiting bonds so we can pursue the greater things that lie before us in our lives.

Dr. Myles Munroe wrote:

> *Prayer is the greatest opportunity and privilege offered to a person in Christ. Yet because of the power of prayer, the adversary makes it his business to see that the prayers of individuals and churches are ineffective. Satan knows that a church is only as powerful as its prayer life. Therefore, he will use misconceptions about prayer to thwart our prayer potential. These misconceptions are hurdles to overcome as we address the problems that lead to unanswered prayer.*[3]

Surviving by the Skin of Our Teeth

In the fall of 1994 I was an immigrant with an unresolved status in a foreign land. I had an entire folder of postponement letters, written to advise me of adjournment upon adjournment of my scheduled appointments with immigration officials. Typically clad in brown envelopes, the letters were not welcome, and I always opened them with a sizable chunk of trepidation in my heart. Every one freaked me out more than the one before.

But now the dreaded day had finally arrived. No more postponements, no retreat, and certainly no surrender on the part of the authorities. They were going for the jugular. My wife and I had gotten on the Piccadilly line at Green Park in Central London, so we could conveniently alight at terminal 4 at Heathrow, our rendezvous point. This journey usually took between forty-five and sixty minutes, depending on the time of day. On this day it felt like twenty minutes. Time flies when you wish it would stop.

After taking a series of escalators, elevators, and twists and turns through high-security doors and coded entry gates, we each sat in a sparse interview room hewn from the depths of the basement floor. *Could anyone even think down here?* I doubted it. We were in the middle of nowhere. The interview ensued and ended quickly .

Awaiting Her Majesty's Secretary of State's decision, it had been a grueling interview on my end. For the authorities, it was just a fulfillment of the standard operating procedure to establish my eligibility for the UK's cherished "indefinite leave to remain" immigration status.

The odds were against me. I hadn't put up a very compelling case by any stretch of the imagination in the face of British immigration law. To add to my tension, my wife was in the last few weeks of her third trimester with our first child, a son. She had been simultaneously subjected to a similar interview in an adjacent cubicle. "Hadn't these dudes ever read the Scripture that said, 'What God hath put together, let no man put asunder'?" I fumed within myself.

To make matters worse, the lawyer who was familiar with our case had sent a trainee to take his place. Great! That trainee had done a sloppy job representing me. To exacerbate an already distressing situation, the interviewer spoke in a super heavy Irish accent. His ethnicity did not matter as much as the need for clear communication about my future prospects. For all I cared, he could have just as well been of Bangladeshi, Burkinabe, or Brunei descent, as long as he did a professional job and could be well understood. He did do a professional job, but as a recent African immigrant, I had a horrible time making out what this stocky bloke was actually saying during the interview, thanks to his decidedly heavy brogue. I knew no cultures other than my own.

The letters had already advised us that in the event that the Secretary of State's decision went against me, I would be deported on the same night without further ado. I therefore was under no illusions that this was a watershed moment. I will never forget the itinerary of deportation at the hands of the UK's national carrier:

British Airways flight: 069

Time of departure: 00:00 hours

Duration of flight: Eight Hours, twenty minutes

Stopovers: None

Special in-flight requirements: None

Seating designation: Economy

This was serious, as difficult as ever. The only question that was popping around in my vexed brain was, "Will I survive this?" Needless to say, my wife had by this time long thrown in the towel over my situation. I shuddered at the thought of being separated from her only eight weeks shy of our first wedding anniversary. I would never see my son, due to arrive in five weeks, in the flesh. When I thought of this, I had felt myself shrink, probably two sizes down.

There are situations in life that can lucidly clarify the grave difference between mental proceedings and heart realities. In my head, the whole prospect of this imminent deportation made me feel like a little nervous nerd. Yet in my heart, all was not lost. God had rescued others. Perhaps He would do the same for me. I did not care how. I was open to the mystical, the miraculous, even the magical, or a cocktail of all these.

I was worried. If God took much longer coming through in my favor, it would be too late. This difficult experience had strangled the daylights out of me. I felt anxious, but this experience had also forced me to develop new spiritual disciplines in an effort to strengthen and prepare myself. One of those was solitude.

Solitude is often erroneously equated with loneliness, but when practiced, we quickly see how it is different. Let's dig a little deeper. You can be solitary without being lonely. Solitude is a place of empowerment—the birthplace of strength. Ironically, you can be horribly lonely in a crowd, so much so that you just can't wait to escape to a solitary place. That experience can be excruciatingly painful. Solitude is not. Instead, it is calming.

Surviving tough times is often dependent on our ability to turn *bitter* into *sweet* and *pressure* into *power.* This skill cannot be learned sitting around the fireplace, nodding off to Grandpa's latest fanciful tale. Neither is it attained by religiously following the Kardashians or some wannabe on our favorite reality TV series. It is not acquired in the controlled and serene atmosphere of a stained glass cathedral either. You don't get it by perusing the latest self-help best seller or by listening to the greatest inspirational preacher. It is not the mainstay of the highly sophisticated or the wealthy, looking down on "lesser" mortals through rose-tinted glasses. Instead, it is developed slowly in the real-life grind of troubles we experience as we journey through the routines of our everyday lives.

Jack Canfield, the highly acclaimed author and cocreator of the *Chicken Soup for the Soul series* with Janet Switzer, attests to the following:

One of life's realities is that major improvements take time; they don't happen overnight. But because so many of today's products and services promise overnight perfection, we've come to expect instant gratification—and we become discouraged when it doesn't happen. However, if you make a commitment to learning something new every day, getting just a little bit better every day, then eventually—over time—you will reach your goals.

Becoming a master takes time. You have to practice, practice, practice! You have to hone your skills through constant use and refinement. It takes years to have the depth and breadth of experience that produces expertise, insight, and wisdom. Every book you read, every class you take, every experience you have is another building block in your career and your life.[4]

Casualties are inevitable in warfare. And this was a battle. I had been relentlessly praying for a long time. I had mustered all the faith I had in God's ability to provide an answer. Surely heaven heard my frantic pleas for divine intervention.

Wielding a freshly printed document, the officer who had interviewed me earlier walked back into the room, trailed by my flustered wife. The angst etched into her face told our story like no words ever could.

SOLITUDE IS A PLACE OF EMPOWERMENT— THE BIRTHPLACE OF STRENGTH.

Still shrunken in my chair, I regarded the officer malevolently as if he were a lab specimen instead of the man. I had steeled myself for this moment. As he read the decision the Secretary of State (his supervisor) had reached regarding my case, I suddenly realized his grimace was actually his best shot at a smile. He was delivering the favorable tidings! Good news!

"Mister . . . um . . . Ka . . . Kateeba," he began, tilting the document to an angle and pronouncing my African surname as if English were the only language on earth, "I'm pleased to inform you that—" I blanked out.

We were back on the train and about halfway into our return journey when I kind of came round. By the look of the stations, it finally dawned on me that we were heading toward Central London again. *Home?*

"How come we're heading home?" I quickly asked Nicola.

"Why?" she asked.

"Have they determined my fate yet?"

"How d'you mean?" she asked, a little disturbed over my disoriented state.

"Well, I thought you were being interrogated too only a little while ago," I maintained.

"Listen, David," she said, a note of brevity in her voice that I couldn't help noticing. "This was real. Your case was settled. Your relentless praying paid off. The Lord came through in our favor, and the rest is history."

"Are you sure?" I whispered, not wanting to be overheard by other passengers on the train within earshot.

"Positive," came the quick reply. "How else would we be back on the train and returning home? You would have been deported otherwise, remember? When we get home, you can read through the documentation in that folder you're holding in your hand. This was divine intervention."

God had come through. My life was forever changed.

The Payoffs of Relentless Prayer

- Relentless prayer grants us continual access to heaven's

resources, which are superior to all others put together, in bringing solutions and closure to the many troubles that speckle human life. The Word of God says:

Because the foolishness of God is wiser than men, and the weakness of God is stronger than men.

—1 Corinthians 1:25

- Relentless prayer ensures that the communication lines between us and God are kept open. Anyone with even the most basic knowledge of military combat will agree that victory is almost guaranteed if you block, compromise, or cut off the communication lines of your adversary.

- Relentless prayer compromises satan's sway and grip on policies and important matters that affect individuals, families, communities, nations, and people groups all over the world, preventing him from wickedly enjoying and exercising an unbridled upper hand over the lives of all people.

- Relentless prayer has the much-needed effect of sharpening our spiritual sensitivity to the leading, promptings, and directives of the Holy Spirit.

- Relentless prayer reaffirms our faith, building us up and strengthening us by the experiences it grants us.

- Relentless prayer demonstrates our submission to the many commands in the Bible directing us to pray (1 Thess. 5:17).

- Relentless prayer builds up your faith (Jude 20).

- Relentless prayer is requests for angelic intervention and backup to help us in our weak attempts to bring change to the problems we see around us. (See Dan. 9:21–22; 10:12–13.)

- Relentless prayer tempers our wayward desires operating deep within the recesses of our minds, even those of which we are unaware. It tears down the fleshly cravings that would otherwise overtake us because prayer opens a pathway for the Holy Spirit to direct us away from those things.

- Relentless prayer builds a strong spiritual base from which we can better deal with the difficult circumstances and hostile situations that often threaten us. From the position of prayer, we gain a fresh perspective, wisdom, and power to stand in any storm.

- Relentless prayer strengthens our resistance to all disease and ill health, especially when these are of a spiritual origin. Ample scientific research supports this idea.

Famed as the father of positive thinking and as one of the most widely read inspirational writers ever, Norman Vincent Peale shared in his book *The Power of Positive Thinking* that:

Experts in physical health and well-being often utilise prayer in their therapy. Disability, tension, and kindred troubles may result from a lack of inner harmony. It is remarkable how prayer restores the harmonious functioning of body and soul.

A friend of mine, a physiotherapist, told a nervous man to whom he was giving a massage: "God works through my fingers as I seek to relax your physical body, which is the temple of your soul. While I work on your outward being, I want you to pray for God's relaxation inwardly." It was a new idea to the patient, but he happened to be in a receptive mood and he tried passing some peace thoughts through his mind. He was amazed at the relaxing effect this had on him.

Jack Smith, operator of a health club which is patronized by many outstanding people, believes in the therapy of prayer, and uses it. He was at one time a prize fighter, then a lorry-driver, later a taxi-driver, and finally opened his health club. He says that while he probes his patrons for physical flabbiness he also probes for spiritual flabbiness, because, he declares: "You can't get a man physically healthy until you get him spiritually healthy."

One day Walter Huston, the actor, sat by Jack Smith's desk. He noted a big sign on the wall on which were pencilled the following letters: A P R P B W P R A A. In surprise Huston asked: "What do those letters mean?"

Smith laughed and said: "They stand for 'Affirmative Prayers Release Powers By Which Positive Results Are Accomplished.'"

Huston's jaw dropped in astonishment. "Well, I never expected to hear anything like that in a health club."

"I use methods like that," said Smith, "to make people curious so they will ask what those letters mean. That gives me an opportunity to tell them that I believe affirmative prayers always get results."

Jack Smith, who helps men to keep physically fit, believes that prayer is as important, if not more important, than exercise, steam baths, and a rub down. It is a vital part of the power-

releasing process.[5]

- Relentless prayer fills us with the power of God and gives us a stronger sense of closeness with God, which in turn renews our confidence and trust in Him to help us withstand anything that threatens our well-being. (See James 5:16.)

- Relentless prayer continually cleanses our conscience. It is impossible to live in guilt and condemnation while engaging in a compelling prayerful life. (See Luke 11:4.)

CHAPTER 2

RECIPROCAL PROMISING

*And Jephthah made a vow to the L*ORD*, and said, "If You will indeed deliver the people of Ammon into my hands, then it will be that whatever comes out of the doors of my house to meet me, when I return in peace from the people of Ammon, shall surely be the L*ORD*'s, and I will offer it up as a burnt offering.*

—Judges 11:30–31

Jephthah was a guy who seemed as if he woke on the wrong side of the bed of life. Before he was born, his mother was working the streets in the red-light district of town where Gilead, his father, met her. After a few close encounters of the adult kind, Gilead decided to take her home and soon passed her off as his second homemaker. However, it's hard to keep that kind of secret in a small town, and it wasn't long before she was being ostracized there.

The community and Gilead's other wife considered her

unwelcome. To them, she was a clear and present danger, not only in the Gilead household but everywhere. Seen in that light, she was treated badly. She wondered whether these finger-pointing holier-than-thou neighbors didn't have their own dried-up skeletons in their closets.

Being the streetwise lass that she was, she did her best to take their unkind treatment in stride, hoping that someday someone would realize that everyone had a past and needed another chance—if only so we could right our wrongs. The "f-word" came into play: forgiveness.

It wasn't long before she became pregnant and delivered a bouncing baby boy. In typical Semitic tradition, she named him with her future prospects, her prevailing circumstances and her emotional state in mind. Fortunately, she still had faith when she did this. She still thought that her big break would come, that God would open doors of opportunity, doors of favor, doors of increase—hence the name Jephthah. From the beginning, baby Jeph looked gorgeous and had a temperament that matched his good looks.

WE ALL HAVE A PAST AND DESERVE ANOTHER CHANCE—IF ONLY SO WE CAN RIGHT OUR WRONGS.

Daftly, Gilead had brought Jephthah's mother home when he already had a wife. This was a recipe for fierce domestic vendettas. Life under Mr. Gilead's roof was not exactly idyllic from that moment on because he had needlessly embroiled his entire household in a competitive and hurtful marriage situation.

As is often the case, the children in Gilead's household were cast into the deep end of a survival-of-the-fittest conflict, and Jephthah enjoyed no immunity in it. He had to grow up in a home where contention and strife were commonplace—so much so that any serene moment was ironically awkward and unnerving as well as infrequent. Chaos was the norm. Tranquility was not.

Even though he was not hated by everyone, Jephthah was raised in a culture that considered women lesser than men and showed no lenience toward them in the event of a faux pas, let alone if they were proved guilty of actual wrongdoing.

By the time Jephthah's stepbrothers had grown up, they were fed up with having to fight in close quarters, so they escalated their childhood brawling into other circles. One day they ganged up on Jephthah and demanded he leave, reminding him in no uncertain terms that he had no inheritance in his father's house because he was "the son of another woman" (Judg. 11:2). This was the straw that broke the camel's back.

Outnumbered and unable to defend himself, Jeph defected to the little-known land of Tob. There he was joined by a band of lowlifes. They became his partners in crime—living off of the loot they took from their poor, unwitting victims.

From Face-Off to Standoff

Every human possesses an innate and enduring reserve of strength and resilience by which they can overcome a whole load of adversity. Albert Einstein once said, "Great spirits have often overcome violent opposition from mediocre minds."[1]

Greatness of spirit is a God-given virtue, but it can sometimes be tricky to discern among the self-effacing, reserved, unassuming, introverted, or melancholy personalities. As a result, these people are often underestimated, despised, or misunderstood. You would be well-advised to steer clear of such a prejudice. As the adage says, "Never judge a book by its cover." Translated loosely, a Ugandan proverb says this: "Never despise that which is coiled up."

Jesus thought the truth found in Psalm 118:22–23 was so important that He posed this question:

> Have you never read in the Scriptures: "The stone which the builders rejected has become the chief cornerstone. This was the Lord's doing, and it is marvelous in our eyes"?
>
> —Matthew 21:42

Like many of us, Jephthah did not realize that *the troubles he grew up with were training*. This hostile household honed his survival instincts, built his moral muscle, and formed the character he'd require when his future opened up later on. In time he emerged with enough strength to nearly single-handedly mastermind the face-off with the Ammonites—the enemies of his kinsmen. He was a true fighter, but even better, he had developed the resilience necessary to bounce back if he ever lost.

You see, strong things are only great for as long as they hold it all together. After that, they fall apart and are no longer considered strong. Resilience makes a person flexible enough to bend and bounce back, as if nothing untoward ever happened. I don't know about you, but I would rather be resilient. *The American Heritage Dictionary of the English Language* says *resilience* is "marked by the ability to recover readily, as from misfortune."[2]

In our story in Judges, after impassioned talks are held and compelling quotas are agreed upon with the elders of Gilead, "The Spirit of the LORD came upon Jephthah" (Judg. 11:29), and he subdued the Ammonites in a faceoff, swinging the pendulum of power in Israel's favor. However, before he did this, he made this vow to God:

> *If You will indeed deliver the people of Ammon into my hands, then it will be that whatever comes out of the doors of my house to meet me, when I return in peace from the people of Ammon, shall surely be the LORD's, and I will offer it up as a burnt offering.*
>
> *—Judges 11:30–31*

This vow turned out to be the worst Jephthah could have made as his daughter came out to greet him. Did he expect an enemy to come from his home? Possibly. However, Jephthah remains an example of a man who stood for the Lord in a time of great trouble for his people, a man of faith.

A Gory Godsend

Sometimes God is revealed best in the gory details of a trial. God's most endearing attributes come into their own when life's grimmest realities raise their ugly heads. God's shepherding is most evident when we are trying to find our way in the wake of our disappointments. If for no other reason, this is because He is needed most at these times.

The devil always hides in the details too. Psalm 46 says:

> *God is our refuge and strength [mighty and impenetrable], a very present and well-proved help in trouble.*
>
> *—Psalm 46:1, AMP, emphasis added*

I often encounter people whose attitude is that God is dispensable. They think they don't really need Him and they can make it on their own. I pray for them because that attitude is nearsighted at best and shows a lack of experience with real trouble in their lives. Real trouble can bring the most fervent atheist to the realization that God is alive and desperately needed in every nook and cranny of life. Whether these people know it or not, trouble is right around the corner on its way to them. It just hasn't knocked at their door yet. And I'm not being melodramatic either. I know from firsthand experience that "in the world you will have tribulation" (John 16:33). As we just read in the psalms, God has a proven track record in helping us out in the nick of time, just when He is most needed.

Hebrews says:

> *Let us therefore come boldly to the throne of grace, that we may obtain mercy and find grace to help in time of need.*

—Hebrews 4:16

It is almost as though mercy and grace can't be obtained apart from times of need. What better way to see God as merciful and gracious than then? How else do you get to know Him as the rescuer unless you are found hanging on to dear life, dangling hopelessly in a precarious situation in which only He can save you? How else does He strike you as a Provider unless you are found needy and only He comes and bails you out?

Can you really speak from firsthand experience that He is Healer if you have never been ill and explored all that medicine and nature had to offer, and He came through and healed you? Can God be the Waymaker to one who's not lost? Isn't He the Deliverer only when He frees us from a bondage that has defied all other avenues?

GOD'S MOST ENDEARING ATTRIBUTES COME INTO THEIR OWN WHEN LIFE'S GRIMMEST REALITIES RAISE THEIR UGLY HEADS.

There are times when God even instigates tough situations! He does this because people seem to learn more in the classroom of pain and suffering than they do any other way. Brian Tracy and Christina Tracy Stein note as follows:

Humans seem to learn only from suffering. Pain is inevitable and unavoidable. But what is really unfortunate is when people experience the pain but fail to identify the lesson that goes with it, which makes it far more likely that they will repeat the mistake that led to the pain.[3]

In such times it is all too easy to blame anything and anyone other than the correct party. In some church circles the devil is blamed for everything at the drop of a hat. On this basis, a spurious spirituality is dialed in, followed by a fascinating array of religious rituals – all in the name of countering another supposed bout of the devil's vicious attacks. They make this judgment because whatever happened bore a strong resemblance to the usual hallmarks of the devil's diabolical modus operandi.

I have been to gatherings that even adopt particular songs and hymns as their anthems—go-to battle cries that will do "the magic" because they assert that "times of difficulty are times of heightened alert." Some employ special slogans like fire up their sleeves, waiting in "ready" mode for the opportune moment to expunge any lingering demons and annihilate the stubborn devil to a degree he has never before fathomed. Others think that if they admit to their failing faith and waning hope in times of suffering, they are doing God a disservice. To avoid that, they soldier on and keep up appearances and begin to act funny, as if they weren't already behaving spooky enough.

In all of this, they fail to perceive that God in His sovereign wisdom already saw the next phase of their lives and had determined and chosen which spell of suffering and training camp of hardship would best prepare them for it. They do not realize that their elevation in life is always commensurate with their tolerance of pain. So instead of avoiding pain, they are better off embracing it and developing a tolerance. Nobody can dodge or escape the lessons God has ordered anyway! Smooth seas never make great sailors!

In the Old Testament we find a prime example of this in the life of Job. After a protracted season of hardship and calamity, he recognized that God must have instigated these ghastly experiences and was up to something greater than he could understand. In referring to God, Job said:

> Look, I go forward, but He is not there, and backward, but I cannot perceive Him; when He works on the left hand, I cannot behold Him; when He turns to the right hand, I cannot see Him. But He knows the way that I take; **when He has tested me, I shall come forth as gold.**
>
> —*Job 23:8–10, emphasis added*

Now, here is a guy who was not going to go down without a fight. He fought for his freedom with all the bravado he could muster. Just like us—his modern-day counterparts—Job thought he could cover all the bases by pushing for escape in a 360-degree spin. He tried to escape his pain when he sensed a long-awaited break, but he simply could not put his finger on the exact place from which it would come. Sadly, this was met with a checkmate, which only served to frustrate him more.

The pain of being stuck in a trial of any kind is twofold: first, there's the fact that you are *almost there*. All your senses seem to attest to how near you are to your breakthrough. You can practically touch it. Your perspective has changed somehow, and that seems to suggest that you are well on your way out of your distress. You hear stuff that says, "You are close. It's almost over." You feel that you are ready to move forward, so you are loaded for bear, pushing forward for your breakthrough. You try going forward, then backward, then to the left, then to the right until you realize that this time around you are stuck and it is not the devil you are dealing with, but God.

SMOOTH SEAS NEVER MAKE GREAT SAILORS!

God is working in you "both to will and to do for His good pleasure" (Phil. 2:13). It becomes clear that you are not going to progress any further than you are willing to be purged. So you must make a promise to God in return, as God has already made good on His promises. He's got your back covered while you travel through this trouble-peppered life.

You also note that your lack of control over your state heightens your bitterness. Your situation cannot be changed, and it is almost a slam dunk that something must die, and Murphy's Law is sure to loom large in your life. This feeling occurs in all kinds of situations: Perhaps you have been caring for a sick family member, and while you are with that person, he or she receives a bone-chilling prognosis. You are immediately a disaster. Perhaps you lost the job you counted on. Perhaps the thing you hoped to do has been cut off by God. Trusting Him in these times is hard.

The Ramah Saga

The countryside where the rounded mountains of Ephraim spread out near the village of Ramah was the setting in which another polygamous household played host to a fierce duel. The underdog was Hannah, who ironically was also her husband Elkanah's real love, but her rival, Peninnah, was the favorite because she had children, while Hannah had none.

As was probably typical of Hebrew women, neither of these feuding women was about to give in to the other. Unbeknownst to them, God had instigated Hannah's barrenness. He would use her trial. With it God would manufacture her testimony of His greatness and faithfulness to His people, even when they hit the darkest threads of the tapestry of life. God was carefully knitting together a beautiful piece of apparel and embellishing it with the scars Hannah had received from Peninnah. Hannah, who had only known ridicule and petty derision, would wear her cloak with mature grace.

And I'm not just making this up as I go along. There are still cultures out there today in which childbearing is the biggest deal ever for a woman. Having a baby is the credential upon which acceptance in those societies is built. A barren woman is a disgrace of cardinal proportions, deserving of the vilest backlash such cultures can mete out.

However, Hannah's long-awaited break came when she stood her ground and made a vow that God found so irresistible that "the LORD remembered her. So it came to pass in the process of time that Hannah conceived and bore a son, and called his name Samuel, saying, 'Because I have asked for him from the LORD'" (1 Sam. 1:19–20).

What was her vow?

> *Then she made a vow and said, "O Lᴏʀᴅ of hosts, if You will indeed look on the affliction of Your maidservant and remember me, and not forget Your maidservant, but will give Your maidservant a male child, **then I will give him to the Lᴏʀᴅ all the days of his life, and no razor shall come upon his head.**"*
>
> *—1 Samuel 1:11, emphasis added*

Miracle secured. What's next?

If God should deliver you from the spiky grip of tough times, what will you do in response? How will your new choices line up with His character? Exactly what are you promising to give up? What guilty pleasures are you going to confess and quit cold turkey? People will always be people. The question therefore is, from now on, how will you handle your relationships? Should this long-standing pain be healed, how will others benefit from your experience?

If you were Jephthah and God delivered you from an adversary like the Ammonites, what promise would you offer as a sweet-smelling sacrifice? That promise is the key to successfully surviving your trials.

YOU ARE NOT GOING TO PROGRESS ANY FURTHER THAN YOU ARE WILLING TO BE PURGED.

Acts 3 relates the story of a man who was off to a pretty tough life from birth. At the mercy of well-wishers and volunteers, this unnamed lame beggar was customarily carried along the streets and placed at the most strategic points available in town, not the least of which was the temple gate called Beautiful. There he was positioned for his long-overdue big break.

The big break actually did come when, at the command of Peter, his crippled legs, feeble knees, and weak ankles suddenly received the strength to leap, walk, and jump! With the miracle secured, guess where he headed?

> So he, leaping up, stood and walked and **entered the temple with them**—walking, leaping, and praising God.
>
> —*Acts 3:8, emphasis added*

What does your next stop become once the key fob dangling in your car is a Lexus or a Mercedes? These items considered evidence of blessing (nice cars, expensive clothing and jewelry, and beautiful homes) do not redefine you. They actually amplify who you've always been.

In the morbid and haunted environs of a cemetery by a hillside dubbed the Gadarenes, which is tucked away on the other side of the Sea of Galilee, lived a once-upon-a-time influential young man, whose scar-speckled body attested to the rough and violent treatment he endured at the hands of his spiritual captors: Legion.

He'd been living there for a considerable time, during which all avenues of redress to the complex spiritual issues about him had been explored and exhausted by relatives and friends to no avail. His mental illness was the result of a six thousand–strong horde of powerful, territorial demonic spirits that had placed him in solitary confinement in this graveyard. The man was in a tough spot until Jesus of Nazareth docked on the shore.

THE THINGS TOUTED AS EVIDENCE OF BLESSING NOWADAYS ... HARDLY REDEFINE YOU. THEY ACTUALLY AMPLIFY WHO YOU'VE ALWAYS BEEN.

The brief face-off between Jesus and the evil spirits that had long besieged this poor soul left even the most fervent skeptic with no doubt as to who the King of all kings and Lord of all lords was. The Nazarene emerged matchless in power and authority. With the assailing spirits expunged and the man's sanity restored, the miracle was secured. Where to next?

In stark contrast to this man's modern-day counterparts when met with a miracle, the Gospel of Mark records this:

> And when He [Jesus] got into the boat, he who had been demon-possessed begged Him [Jesus] that he might be with Him.
>
> —Mark 5:18

This desire on the part of the man to be with Jesus is quite remarkble considering that his influence before his psychopathic meltdown spanned a ten-city scope—the Decapolis. In the aftermath of healing, the natural inclination for anyone in this man's position would have been to head speedily back to his own neighborhood to resume business where he left off, right? Wrong. The correct thing to do was to beg to stay and, if necessary, cling tight to Jesus, the Deliverer by whom his liberty and freedom had been regained.

Fixing What Should Fail

You really don't want to be found trying to fight the process and fix what God has decided should fail. Thanks to the tardiness of humanity in catching on to this paradox of life, it's always much later that we finally get to appreciate that what we thought was a bad situation was *de facto* a godsend after all—that our experience was gory, yes, but a godsend nonetheless. Quinine tastes horrible, but it deals with malaria fairly and squarely. Nasty, but nourishing; excruciating, but edifying; bitter, but beneficial—the distress was destiny in disguise. Writes Raymond Holliwell:

> *Each experience through which we pass operates ultimately for our good. This is a correct attitude to adopt and we must be able to see it in that light.*[4]

Isn't it interesting how we like to be noted as experienced in our field of expertise yet passionately loathe having to recall the very experiences by which we got there?

At an awards ceremony for his film directing and stellar

performance in the 2016 blockbuster movie *Fences*, the Hollywood stalwart Denzel Washington received a standing ovation and several accolades. In his acceptance speech, he proffered words of encouragement to the young and upcoming artists, admonishing them not to give up their dreams of making it to stardom in the face of hardship. He concluded by making a profound statement that is in keeping with the gist of the foregoing truths: "Ease is a greater threat to progress than hardship."[5]

Stop for a moment and lay aside whatever fears or reservations you might have about that statement. You cannot improve your life in an environment where you are at ease. You need some kind of pressure, born out of adversity, to begin to act in a manner that propels you into the desirable future that waits on the other side of your trial. Pressure, however, should not be confused with stress.

YOU CANNOT CHANGE OR IMPROVE YOUR LIFE IN AN ENVIRONMENT WHERE YOU ARE AT EASE.

Stress is a definite no-no. Pressure and hardship have an uncanny way of churning the cream out of us and challenging even the most dormant among us to rise to the occasion of new opportunities so we can become more productive and do greater things.

God did not mince His words when He spoke to the people of Jerusalem in the days of the prophet Zephaniah.

> *And it shall come to pass at that time that I will search Jerusalem with lamps, and punish the men who are settled in complacency, who say in their heart, "The LORD will not do good, nor will He do evil."*
>
> —*Zephaniah 1:12*

Sometimes suffering serves to prepare us for a higher purpose and plan, while ease can ironically be in direct opposition to that greater purpose. Jesus is a perfect example of this. One would think that God should have spared His Son the burden of suffering considering that Jesus was always in sync with His Father's ways, will, and wisdom, but instead, we learn from the writer of Hebrews:

> *Though He was a Son, yet **He learned obedience by the things which He suffered**. And having been perfected, He became the author of eternal salvation to all who obey Him.*
>
> —*Hebrews 5:8–9, emphasis added*

You see, obedience is a learned thing. It is a derivative of nurture, *not* nature. It is for everyone, even those born with the proverbial silver spoon in their mouth. No one has a natural tendency toward obedience. Quite the reverse. Suffering is therefore God's choice vehicle by which we are molded into shape and through which our hearts and attitude are made more pliable and changed.

Of Christ's suffering John MacArthur writes:

> *Jesus was executed as a criminal on a cross. Yet He was guilty of no crime—no wrong, no trespass, no sin. He never*

had an evil thought or spoke an evil word. His was the most unjust execution ever perpetrated on a human being. Yet from it we learn that though a person may be perfectly within the will of God—greatly loved and gifted, perfectly righteous and obedient—he may still experience unjust suffering. Like Jesus, he may be misunderstood, misrepresented, hated, persecuted, and even murdered. In His death Christ set the standard of how to respond to unjust persecution.[6]

When you experience suffering, you soon realize that you are not as smart as you thought. Suffering has a strange way of instilling critical and indispensable values that we probably wouldn't get by any other means.

Writing to Timothy, his son in the faith, Paul made this clarion call:

You therefore must endure hardship as a good soldier of Jesus Christ.

—2 Timothy 2:3

The Christian life is not nearly as much a sprint as it is a test of endurance. As in a marathon, it is your longevity and steadfastness that matters. Staying the course and personal stamina, not the speed of your ambitions, are most important.

Viktor E. Frankl says:

There are situations in which one is cut off from the opportunity to do one's work or to enjoy one's life; but what never can be ruled out is the unavoidability of suffering. In accepting this challenge to suffer bravely, life has a meaning up to the last moment, and it retains this meaning literally to the end. In other words, life's meaning is an unconditional one, for it even includes the potential meaning of unavoidable suffering.[7]

I hope that this ministers to someone who thinks salvation exonerates us from suffering. Salvation solidifies us for eternity, but it does not make us immune from suffering. Salvation empowers us to endure suffering with a sense of hope that things will turn out well in the end because God has us covered. Our hope enables us to stand and stare suffering in the face, fearlessly declaring, "Bring it on, loser. I know whose I am."

Hardship (just like blessing) comes to all people—the sinner and the saint, the nice and the nasty, the godly and the ghastly. If this truth is anything like salt, let me rub a few more pinches of it into the wound with the following examples.

Joe

Joe was a happy-go-lucky lad. He was born and raised in an affluent and godly Jewish family in the picturesque hinterland of Hebron. He was papa's boy too, so he had great confidence and a zest for life that anyone in his position would have. He bordered on being spoiled because of the preferential treatment he received from his dad, who made him special, colorful outfits, which he wore with pride. This favoritism so incited the envy and displeasure of his eleven elder brothers that they eventually had had enough and cooked up a nasty plot to put Joe in his rightful place. He was obviously getting too big for his boots.

The fact that Joe frequently recounted his dreams of superiority over his brothers, even though he was only seventeen and they were all older than he was, just added fuel to the already smoldering fire and bolstered their resolve to get rid of this youngster in any way possible. And get rid of him they did.

Joe narrowly escaped death at the hands of his incensed brothers, thanks to the timely intervention of Reuben, the eldest and most rational of them all. However, the sinister agenda of most of the brothers was unknown even to Reuben, and in time Joe found himself in an arid pit in the wilderness. The brothers feigned his death to Jacob, their father, brandishing Joe's shredded and blood-drenched multicolored robe as evidence.

In a fascinating twist of events, Joe found himself in Africa—sold into slavery in Egypt to the captain of the head of state's armed guard for twenty shekels of silver. Through all this suffering, it was not immediately clear that God still cared. And yet He actually stayed so close to Joe that even those around the young man couldn't help but acknowledge the sure and steadfast behind-the-scenes handiwork of a powerful and awesome deity in his life. The Bible says:

> The LORD was with Joseph, and he was a successful man; and he was in the house of his master the Egyptian. And his master saw that the LORD was with him and that the LORD made all he did to prosper in his hand. So Joseph found favor in his sight, and served him. Then he made him overseer of his house, and all that he had he put under his authority.
>
> —Genesis 39:2–4

Whenever I read these verses, I often wondered why it says, "The LORD was with Joseph, and he was a successful man" against the backdrop of betrayal, blackmail, and the close call Joseph had suffered at the hands of his baleful blood brothers. Surely this Lord who was behind Joseph's success and blessings was capable enough to save the poor lad from all this. And surely it would all come out and he would regain his place next.

This bent in me was deeply ingrained, a religious, yet incorrect, assumption that surmised that suffering was a punishment reserved only for the unspiritual, unrepentant, and ungodly.

SOMETIMES SUFFERING SERVES TO PREPARE YOU FOR A HIGHER PURPOSE.

However, biblical evidence coupled with my own experience began to knock down these sacred cows I had been breeding. I learned that sometimes God's salvation comes to us at an angle. Sometimes the timing is offbeat, and often His deliverance wears a mask we do not recognize or understand.

In the heat of our suffering, our theology can make us blind at the very time when, in the grand scheme of things, God is masterfully weaving together a beautiful end. Sharon Salzberg puts it this way:

When I'm at the ragged edge of an anxious night, when I've tried hard to help someone and am drained by frustration and grief, when the suffering I encounter threatens to pull me down into futility, I need to begin by reminding myself of what I am not seeing in the picture of suffering right before me.[8]

Sometimes all we actually need is the presence of God to relieve the sting of our hardship and pain. With Him we gain help to walk through the trouble and grow in it. We do not die as we thought we would.

We also wise up. We learn that if we are to survive similar quagmires, it is necessary that we develop filters that allow only the qualified to access the inner sanctums of our souls, where our dreams and visions live, so they can continue to grow nurtured and protected. Those whom we consider our confidants must first pass a litmus test. They must prove themselves having the intellectual and spiritual maturity required to handle our dreams with care and tenderness, as well as discretion.

Mr. and Mrs. J.

Although we've already gleaned some truths from examples in the life of Mr. J., so rich in content is his story that it merits revisiting—this time with the Mrs. in the picture.

The very first verse of the first chapter of the book of Job makes for a pretty impressive introduction.

There was a man in the land of Uz, whose name was Job; **and that man was blameless and upright, and one who feared God and shunned evil.**

—*Job 1:1, emphasis added*

Mr. J. was a shrewd investor and an astute entrepreneur. To say that he was loaded is an understatement. If he lived in our day, he would have had an assortment of paid-for Lamborghinis and Ferraris, a custom-made Maybach, a Rolls-Royce stretch limousine for good measure, and a Bentley convertible to complete the lineup. For now we'll save the detailing of his airplanes for another time. The point is that Job was rich, filthy rich.

A private boulevard elegantly flanked by stately palm trees led to his palace; colorful flowers composed his gardens where exotic animals and birds lived happily.

His wardrobe came straight from Paris and the salons of designers such as Louis Vuitton, Yves Saint Laurent, Tommy Hilfiger, Michael Kors, Calvin Klein, and Thomas Burberry, unless it had been flown in from their Italian counterparts: Fendi, Giorgio Armani, Versace, Prada, Roberto Cavalli, Dolce & Gabbana, and Gucci. Rolex watches and diamond jewelry from Harry Winston, Swarovsky, Graff, Tiffany, and Bulgari adorned his family.

Enter Mrs. J. She was a glamorous and beautiful woman who enjoyed her life. With the snap of a finger, her every need was supplied. In a houseful of livery-clad domestic staff that included chefs, a top drawer personal assistant, a team of nannies and masseuses, butlers, a couple of chauffeurs, and several top-notch security personnel with bulbous biceps, she lived a life of ease and plenty.

Mrs. J. often visited her villa in Tuscany when she wanted to get away, but every so often she went off in her luxury yacht to Hawaii instead—that is, when she felt it was all right to leave Mr. J. on his own.

But now, fasten your seat belt as we begin our descent and prepare to land in a place where you'll be quickly snapped back to reality. I hope you enjoyed your time in fantasyland in the life of the Job family, an odyssey in which you were introduced to the opulence that could have marked their living experience, had they been our contemporaries. I painted this imaginary picture to drive a point home. (Hopefully the picture was clear.)

I once herded my father's twelve cattle and shepherded his six goats and four sheep at the peak of his ranching career, which made Dad the greatest of all in his clan back in the day, so I take my hats off to Job, whose livestock inventory boasted seven thousand sheep and:

> *Three thousand camels, five hundred yoke of oxen, five hundred female donkeys, and a very large household, so that this man was the greatest of all the people of the East.*
>
> *—Job 1:3*

Given this profile, we can see that Job knew no suffering or hardship, but his wealth did not give him any immunity. The glowing account of his attributes in the introduction is short-lived because he is devastated by the thirteenth verse of the same chapter when disaster mercilessly strikes. Thereafter, we are staggered by the debacles that unfold in Job's life, regardless of his wealth, blamelessness, and upright behavior. This father of ten is hurled headlong into a series of ferocious satanic attacks that leave him lying in the dust, stricken but unfazed in his faith and loyalty to God.

He was still a happy man. A happy man's moods are never based on the circumstances around him. A happy man deliberately chooses not to place the responsibility of his emotional well-being on anything or anyone else but himself. Neither will he expect only favorable circumstances in life. Job's character had been built by God.

Marci Shimoff writes this:

Many people in Western culture are striving for success. They want the great home, they want their businesses to work, they want all these outer things. But what we found in our research is that having these outer things does not necessarily guarantee what we really want, which is happiness. So we go for these outer things thinking they're going to bring us happiness, but it's backward. You need to go for the inner joy, the inner peace, the inner vision first, and then all of the outer things appear.[9]

In the Bible, we are told that:

In all this Job did not sin nor charge God with wrong.

—Job 1:22

As time goes on, Job somehow stands steadfast, declaring that:

For I know that my Redeemer lives, and He shall stand at last on the earth; and after my skin is destroyed, this I know, that in my flesh I shall see God, whom I shall see for myself, and my eyes shall behold, and not another. How my heart yearns within me!

—Job 19:25–27

Mr. J. knows that whatever is happening to him and his family is a test that will be short-lived. It has an expiration date. He is confident that God saw the coming tsunami of trouble that has befallen him and was not caught off guard. Instead God allowed it to happen, knowing that He had Job's back covered. Job trusted that. It's no wonder, then, that only four chapters later he declares what he knows to be true:

> But He [God] knows the way that I take; when He has tested me, I shall come forth as gold.
>
> —Job 23:10

And come forth as gold Job does. He survives. His story ends on a pretty positive note too.

> Indeed the LORD gave Job twice as much as he had before. . . . Now the LORD blessed the latter days of Job more than his beginning. . . . After this Job lived one hundred and forty years, and saw his children and grandchildren for four generations. So Job died, old and full of days.
>
> —Job 42:10, 12, 16–17

Zach and Lizzy

Zach was a personable chap. Lizzy, his childhood sweetheart, even more so. The duo had earned themselves the coveted reputation of being the most devout couple in their deeply religious neighborhood, with their graceful aging added to the tally of merits already going for them.

Theirs was an unwavering commitment to the service of God in their church. Zach had proudly worn his priestly attire for decades, but there was an Achilles' heel, and a baffling one at that, in their story: These two lovebirds, now rather old, were childless.

HAPPY PEOPLE'S MOODS ARE NEVER BASED ON THEIR CIRCUMSTANCES. NEITHER WILL THEY EXPECT ONLY FAVORABLE CIRCUMSTANCES IN LIFE.

Whereas fertility issues befall either gender, Jewish cultural norms bestowed the gravest blame on the female in such cases, and Lizzy, who ironically hailed from a pretty spiritual lineage, was accordingly ticketed as the black sheep.

It is a shame that Zach and Lizzy's story doesn't command much confidentiality by now and Luke, who is not exactly tacit, probably owing to the eye for detail that any other physician of his caliber would sport, even makes it public domain when he writes thus:

There was in the days of Herod, the king of Judea, a certain priest named Zacharias, of the division of Abijah. His wife was of the daughters of Aaron, and her name was Elizabeth. And they were both righteous before God, walking in all the commandments and ordinances of the Lord blameless. But

*they had no child, because Elizabeth was barren, and they
were both well advanced in years.*

—Luke 1:5–7

Notice that this couple's integrity doesn't go unnoticed by the writer. We know we're talking about folks who are famed for following God's Word to the letter—folks whose righteousness and blamelessness before God were so impressive that it was chronicled in Scripture. These virtues, however, neither exonerated them from the misery of barrenness nor earned them any exemption from hardship.

Despite their deep spirituality, brother Zach and sister Lizzy were not automatically insulated against the reproach that any other regular person, presumably more unrighteous, would suffer. However, in time they did survive this tough time in their journey, thanks to an angelic intervention masterminded by God, which allowed Lizzy to conceive and bear baby John in her old age.

THE CHRISTIAN LIFE IS NOT NEARLY AS MUCH A SPRINT AS IT IS A MARATHON.

Paul

Paul was a survivor and an audacious go-getter. In his zeal, Paul delivered on any commitment he made, even if his own life hung in the balance. He was an unflinching hard-liner, and he didn't just talk the talk. He also walked the walk. His pragmatic, daring, and proactive stance, along with his brazen approach to life, made him a frequent presence in the flurry of trouble that doggedly stalked. But on the bright side, his example of faith and faithfulness is pervasive throughout the book of Acts, especially from the thirteenth chapter all the way through to the end of the book.

Writing three quarters of the New Testament was by no means an easy feat, especially when most of it was written while he was imprisoned, as Paul served time in many Roman jails, complete with fetters, shackles, and chains used for the inmates. Paul had to win his spurs in all circumstances.

So impressive is Paul's résumé that attempting to lay it out here would simply be a travesty of epic proportions, so let's hear it from the horse's mouth:

Are they Hebrews? So am I. Are they Israelites? So am I. Are they the seed of Abraham? So am I. Are they ministers of Christ?—I speak as a fool—I am more: in labors more abundant, in stripes above measure, in prisons more frequently, in deaths often. From the Jews five times I received forty stripes minus one. Three times I was beaten with rods; once I was stoned; three times I was shipwrecked; a night and a day I have been in the deep; in journeys often, in perils of waters, in perils of robbers, in perils of my own countrymen, in perils of the Gentiles, in perils in the city, in perils in the wilderness, in perils in the sea, in perils among false brethren; in weariness and toil, in sleeplessness often, in hunger and thirst, in fastings often, in cold and nakedness—besides the other things, what comes

upon me daily: my deep concern for all the churches. Who is
weak, and I am not weak? Who is made to stumble, and I do
not burn with indignation? If I must boast, I will boast in the
things which concern my infirmity.

—2 Corinthians 11:22–30

If nothing else, at least we see here that Paul commands comeback power. When he makes the reciprocal promise that he will boast in the things that concern his infirmity, it's almost as though he's heard motivational speaker and life coach Les Brown say, "When life knocks you down, try to land on your back. Because if you can look up, you can get up."[10]

One day when I grow up and I'm allowed to do so, I will add that "if you can get up, then you can survive tough times!" Actually even if I'm not allowed, I'll say it anyway.

CHAPTER 3

REASSURING PROFESSION

Let no corrupt word proceed out of your mouth, but what is good for necessary edification, that it may impart grace to the hearers.

—Ephesians 4:29

Words have power. Yes, they possess power of great magnitude. They carry the power to blight and the power to build, the power to bruise and the power to bless. They have the power to mar and the power to mend. They have the power to hurt and the power to heal. They have so much power that we owe the very existence of our world to them. The creative power of words is actually responsible for the universe and all its galaxies the way we know them today. In no better place is the power of words showcased than in the story of creation, where the Creator spoke the creation into being.

Millennia later, the Gospel of John presents the words that were spoken by God as a person in creation. Now words have literally taken on a persona of their own—an entity personified in Jesus Christ. We read this:

> In the beginning was **the Word**, and **the Word** was with God, and **the Word** was God. **He** was in the beginning with God. All things were made through **Him**, and without **Him** nothing was made that was made.
>
> —*John 1:1–3, emphasis added*

Graham Powell and Shirley Powell note this of God:

> He rules the entire universe by the power of His word. If He chose to, He could speak one word and the entire universe would be obliterated. Jesus spoke to the wind and the storm and it instantly obeyed Him. He healed and delivered by speaking words. We launch our spiritual weapons through speaking.[1]

Well over two and a half decades of pastoral ministry have left an indelible impression on my heart and taught me a lesson or two about people, their struggles, and the Word of God. I have seen the restoration firsthand of the devastated lives of thousands. They are now whole and placed back into the running through correctly timed, highly anointed, graciously spoken, and consistently repeated positive words.

Inevitably I have in the same period of time also seen countless once-upon-a-time decent souls get utterly shattered, irretrievably broken, cruelly smothered, callously disfigured, and totally maimed by words.

Melanie

As a pastor in the local community, how do you proceed when you visit, as I did, the apartment of Melanie, a single parent whose only teenage son's dear life has been snuffed out in a fatal stabbing only a day earlier, courtesy of a senseless juvenile altercation? You start with reassuring professions, well knowing that you are dealing with a woman for whom time has stood still, whose life has literally hit a complete blackout.

The Word of God in your mouth is as strong as it would be if God were speaking it forth Himself. He rebutted Jeremiah the prophet when the latter cited his youth and oratory flaws thus:

> *"Do not be afraid of their faces, for I am with you to deliver you," says the LORD. Then the LORD put forth His hand and touched my mouth, and the LORD said to me: "Behold, I have put My words in your mouth."*

> *—Jeremiah 1:8–9*

Armed to the teeth with the Word of God, Jeremiah set out for the nations and kingdoms on account of which he'd been ordained. By the utterances he was making, he was able to root out, pull down, destroy, throw down, build, and plant (Jer. 1:10). God said:

> *I have put My words in your mouth; I have covered you with the shadow of My hand, that I may plant the heavens, lay the foundations of the earth, and say to Zion, "You are My people."*

> *—Isaiah 51:16*

Much later we are taken much closer to the bone, as it were, with the words of Jesus. He said:

The words that I speak to you are spirit, and they are life.

—John 6:63

Kayemba

How should I respond to a wee hours phone call in which the subdued voice of Kayemba, a guy I'd known for years, described the heart-wrenching details of his recent divorce from his wife of nine years and the mother of their four kids? He now sought direction. I answered with reassurance, all the while sensitive to the fact that he was in the deep end of the pool. The psalmist said:

Your word is a lamp to my feet and a light to my path.

—Psalm 119:105

So I kept speaking the Word until the reassurances I made caught onto him and he began to see light again.

Martin

In a sad turn of events, Martin, the breadwinner in a family, lost his job. The corporation he worked for was "downsizing," but the reality was that their major firing was the result of a worldwide economic downturn. Who could blame the corporation? After the dust of the financial crisis settled, a whopping $19.2 trillion in the United States alone was wiped out! Starting with Wall Street, thirty-four million jobs were destroyed globally. Martin was only a drop in the ocean of victims.

Still, the implications were far-reaching and not sympathetic to the schooling of Marvin, Mabel, and Miriam, the three kids Martin and Martha, their stay-at-home mother, were raising. Moreover, Miriam, who was born premature and had developed neurological complications, now required a specialist's care. How do you minister to a family that is undoubtedly experiencing a terrible trial? You give them reassurance from the Word of God.

And the Lord will deliver me from every evil work and preserve me for His heavenly kingdom. To Him be glory forever and ever. Amen!

—2 Timothy 4:18

Sangita

I finally hit the sack in the early hours of the new day after a long time of study in preparation of the next morning's worship service. Just to ensure that my sleep was not prematurely interrupted, I set my electronic gizmos to silent mode. I was only human, after all.

Nonetheless, my cell phone alerted me of an incoming message. Talk about timing! I had only slept three hours, so I chose to ignore the call. I reached for the phone to power it down so I could deal with matters when I woke from my much-deserved rest. It powered down, but not before I caught a hazy glimpse of the sender. It was Sangita.

Sangita had never attempted to reach me at such an odd hour. In fact, she called them "unholy hours." She was a mature and cultured parishioner of my congregation. This behavior was very atypical of her. There had to be a good reason for her to breach this rule of thumb. I rebooted my phone and found the message this divorced mother of four sent. Here's what it said:

> Dear pastor,
>
> Please pray for my daughter Vanya in South Africa. She has been admitted to the hospital and is under intensive care with a nervous breakdown. I know that with your earnest prayers, the Lord will move and have mercy upon her. She especially needs this prayer support because she only recently came to the faith, as you know, and is still in the inchoate stages of her spiritual journey. The enemy must be irate about her. Please stand in for her. Thank you very much.

How do you productively respond to Sangita and Vanya's medical juggernaut? You begin with reassurance. You must speak life-giving words to good effect because you are bound by your honor to reciprocate the confidence and faith that Sangita has vested in your intervention. She obviously thinks your prayers command greater sway in the heavenlies. She has probably predicated her thinking on the track record that trails you in such matters. As you toggle between wakefulness and sleep, you write:

> Hello, Sangita,
>
> Message received. Content noted. My heart goes out to you and Vanya. It is well though. Remember 1 Corinthians 10, which categorically states that:
>
> > "No temptation has overtaken you except such as is common

to man; but God is faithful, who will not allow you to be tempted beyond what you are able, but with the temptation will also make the way of escape, that you may be able to bear it" (1 Cor. 10:13).

We'll meet up later and figure out the way of escape from this. In the meantime, angels are on assignment; the Lord cares and has Vanya's back covered.

Pastor David

Brian

Arriving on time at my office for his 11:00 a.m. appointment was Brian, a young man in his late twenties. I did not observe the usual hospitality, and neither did Brian. He poured himself out of all that weighed him down: his secret, but long-standing, struggle with drug abuse. *Oh, not again*, I secretly murmured to myself, hoping he did not pick up on my distress. My eye noted his fidgety mannerisms that told the toll substance abuse was taking on his handsome demeanor. I wanted to help this ailing soul but felt inadequate. His story was unnerving.

Brian started out well, but his life veered when he started hanging out with the wrong peer group, which eventually led him to leave the church. Now his life had finally come to a grinding halt. Typically, the devil was giggling with a diabolical sense of satisfaction at the wreck he had contrived in Brian's life.

It finally occurred to me that the best resource for such cases was the Word of God. I hastily reassured Brian with Scripture:

Let no corrupt word proceed out of your mouth, but what is good for necessary edification, that it may impart grace to the hearers.

—Ephesians 4:29

The Bible says:

Death and life are in the power of the tongue.

—Proverbs 18:21

When I read this, a powerful reality popped out at me. In this paradox, two eternally contrary entities are juxtaposed and made subservient to a third. Death and life remain passive entities until they are impacted by an even greater phenomenon: words. I don't know about you, but that is powerful!

Isn't it amazing that matters as powerful and final as death and life are affected by words? Whether one lives is decided in a courtroom whose presiding justice is words! That tells me that death and life are essentially end results. You are, therefore, an embodiment of the sum total of the words that have been spoken into your life.

When you find yourself in a tough time, the one thing that you probably can't prevent is verbalizing your inner turmoil and sense of helplessness. This inclination to verbally vent your frustration will come at you like an avalanche. If words spoken under sufficient pressure and duress are anything to go by, you may even surprise yourself as to how morally decadent you are—rapidly spewing out words that the not very clean part of your imagination knows well.

For a moment, it might seem as though the use of foul language would magically break apart the dark forces hell-bent on choking the life out of us just as a boa constrictor does with its prey. And trust me, even the saintliest among us uses foul language from time to time. It just happens.

YOU ARE, THEREFORE, AN EMBODIMENT OF THE SUM TOTAL OF THE WORDS THAT HAVE BEEN SPOKEN INTO YOUR LIFE.

However, the Word of God offers an antidote that stands in stark disparity to these futile utterances. Note that the Bible instructs us in Ephesians 4 to not use corrupt speech. Even though you may think all kinds of awful things, you do have control over what you say.

The King James Version renders this verse thus:

> Let no corrupt communication proceed out of your mouth, but that which is good to the use of edifying, that it may minister grace unto the hearers.
>
> —*Ephesians 4:29, KJV*

This tells us that while your mind may *produce* distasteful ideas and grim thoughts, your mouth must neither *pronounce* nor *proclaim* them.

What is corrupt communication? It is my conviction that the

phrase *corrupt communication* refers to any ungracious words—words that are in direct opposition to the will, character, and purposes of God. They are considered corrupt because they don't build up; instead, they tear down a struggling person's hope in God. Rather than ministering grace to the hearer, they actually administer gloom. They are contrary to God's ways and pose a very real threat to a positive outcome in the life of the one going through a trial.

With good reason, negative utterances are sternly discouraged throughout the length and breadth of the Bible. As already stated, this whole universe as we know it came into being thanks to the creative force that attended the positive utterances God made in His seven-day creation spree.

WHILE YOUR MIND MAY PRODUCE OR PROCESS DISTASTEFUL IDEAS AND GRIM THOUGHTS, YOUR MOUTH MUST NEITHER PRONOUNCE NOR PROCLAIM THEM.

In Numbers 13, there is a vivid example of the power and effects of negative words. Here, twelve choice envoys are sent out to spy out the land God promised to the children of Israel. These people were right on the verge of possessing this lovely, yet long overdue, blessing and were waiting with bated breath in the wilderness of

Paran at Kadesh. The envoys returned forty days later.

Bringing huge clusters of grapes, the twelve began to share their lowdown on the Promised Land, making it a point to highlight the mammoth size of the warriors and the huge, fortified cities they found there, comparing these against their own seemingly small strength. This was a great David-versus-Goliath scenario.

The way we repeatedly fail to realize that the grapes we yearn for in life are almost always found where the giants we dread reside reveals something about humans. We fail to count our blessings, yet we find the energy to spend the better part of our days focusing on our gremlins. We lose the moon while counting the stars.

Sandwiched between trusty Hoshea and coy Gaddi, Geuel demurely gestured to Shammua to begin speaking.

"Guys, let me clue you in about this place we explored in the last forty days," started Shammua, clasping his hands together as if that gave him some kind of added oratory confidence. "The land was really beautiful!"

"Well, beauty lies in the eyes of the beholder, you know," interrupted Nahbi. "You're gonna have to be a lot more objective than that."

"Then why don't you go ahead and tell 'em, mister objective?" said Igal in his raspy, deep voice. "The truth is the truth, regardless of how objective any of us claims to be."

"Yep, that's what all our people are waiting to hear," began Shaphat. "Friends!" he continued as he positioned himself to face the attentive, "the whole idea of possessing the Promised Land sucks, to be honest with you. We are going to have to make do with where we're at instead."

"Hey, hey, hey, guys, look!" cried Caleb, with a note of solemnity. "I was right there in the thick of everything. I know we seemed like no match for the big guns we saw there, but just remember how big the Lord has proved Himself all these years. Do you guys really believe that He's gonna abandon us now, when we need Him most? We have come way too far to begin doubting now! I really think we're well able to possess this land. The God of our forefathers is with us."

"Well, I knew you'd say that," said Sethur, "but be reasonable for once, Caleb. I've always wished your bite were as good as your bark. Are you honestly saying that we were anything other than grasshoppers before those beastly behemoths we saw there? Come on, man!"

"Yeah, tell everybody here how you think we'll take possession of those cities with the kind of walls you saw there, Caleb," charged Palti, "and tell 'em the exact plan of attack we'll adopt, 'cause I tell you what, mate, the Benjamites I represent are the least of all, and I'm not about to let any of these poor souls get sacrificed on the altar of your fanciful whims."

Gaddiel cleared his voice as he tightened his grip on the wooden rod resting on his and Ammiel's shoulders, suspending the grapes in midair. "Guys, let's just accept that you win some and you lose some! This time we've actually lost before we even began. There's no way we're gonna possess that land, considering the strength of its residents. Brethren, those dudes are bad, and Ammiel and I are out!"

Maybe you think this reenactment is far-fetched, but it is intended to capture the spirit of what could have transpired as the twelve men returned and spoke to the people waiting. The report relayed back to the attentive audience by those spies (with the exception of Joshua and Caleb) was wildly negative and forceful. The text says:

> So all the congregation lifted up their voices and cried, and the people wept that night. And all the children of Israel complained against Moses and Aaron, and the whole congregation said to them, "If only we had died in the land of Egypt! Or if only we had died in this wilderness! . . . Let us select a leader and return to Egypt."
>
> —Numbers 14:1–2, 4

As a result of the ten spies' report, the Israelite congregation members moaned and were afraid. Instead of meeting the challenge of the Promised Land, they were prepared to appoint a leader who could ensure their safe return to their dismal past.

In life, there are people whose paths you don't want to cross, ones you want to avoid like the plague. These folks will not hesitate to retreat in the face of any challenge. They live a colorless existence and only want leadership that competently steers them in a well-regulated manner. Unfortunately, these people are many among us instead of few.

Purely on account of the negative and positive speeches they made that day in the wilderness of Paran at Kadesh, the story ends on the following intriguing note:

> Now the men whom Moses sent to spy out the land, who returned and made all the congregation complain against

*him by bringing a bad report of the land, those very men who brought the evil report about the land, **died by the plague** before the LORD. **But Joshua the son of Nun and Caleb the son of Jephunneh remained alive,** of the men who went to spy out the land.*

—*Numbers 14:36–38, emphasis added*

The Proof in the Pudding

Results count. It is easy to talk, but until there is proof, all our talk is only pie in the sky. Let us now revisit the stories of Melanie, Kayemba, Martin, Sangita, and Brian.

Now it is just over two years since Melanie's son was laid to rest. Her son's short life is eternally embedded in her memory. Equally so are the words of encouragement I spoke to her at what was arguably the worst moment of her life. She clearly recalls my reassurance from the Word of God and my assertion that "God is ever so faithful. He will personally see to it that you are given double for your trouble." Although that made no sense to her at the time, she held it in her heart.

Six months after that funeral, an unassuming, but intense, suitor showed up. He wooed and won Melanie's slowly healing heart and exchanged marriage vows with her on the first anniversary of her son's death. Since then she and Michael (her husband) have spoken to me about how the words I gave her helped her. Even more, the couple learned they were expecting twins! Three weeks after our visit, she and Michael came home with gorgeous and healthy boy and girl bundles of joy.

. . .

An eleven-seat stretch limousine idled in the courtyard of a beautiful stone village church. Its occupants relaxed in their luxurious environs. A tender drizzle welcomed this glorious Saturday morning, and it finally stopped and gave way to a fresh gentle breeze. Sparrows chirped and goldfinches twittered, adding to the music emanating from the organ inside the church.

The organist suddenly switched to Mendelssohn's wedding march, and the groom stood. Likewise, the best man. Each were flanked by a miniature rendition of themselves played by the groom's two sons; this duo turned to watch the bridal entourage making its grand entrance into the sanctuary, chaperoned by the couple's two equally cute daughters.

The groom and bride exchanged their own unique written vows. The groom's read:

I, Douglas Kayemba, having awoken from my two-year witless stupor, have fallen both irretrievably and hopelessly in love with you after all, and of my own volition and without coercion do hereby retake you, Doreen—my kindred soul, mother of my four gorgeous munchkins, completer of my wants, constant giver, bone of my bone, flesh of my flesh, replenisher of my flickering spirit, companion like no other, warmth of my heart, breath of fresh air, discreet confidant bar none, reason for the spring in my step, and woman of my dreams—to be my awesome, lawful wedded wife from this day forward, to love and to hold . . . 'til death do us part!

It took two years to finally straighten out and annul the divorce process they triggered. I was happy to see the change.

. . .

The phone rang. It was 8:15 a.m. Weary feet headed toward the handset. A calloused palm grabbed it; a cracking voice just managed a "hullo." The caller introduced himself.

"Can I speak with Martin, please?"

"Martin speaking."

"Oh, great. Listen, Martin, our executive board has decided to hire you. I'm pleased to inform you that your contract is already in the mail. When you get it, just fill it out and send it back, and we'll pick up from there."

"Really? That's wonderful!"

My cell phone vibrated at 8:17 a.m. It was Martin. Which prayer haven't I prayed yet with regard to his work situation? Why did he continue to run into dead-ends in looking for a job? I took a deep breath. Then I ignored the call. At 8:18 my phone vibrated, and the display showed that Martin was calling again. I always got cold feet when he called. Finally, there was a text: "You're not going to believe this, pastor! Please get back to me ASAP!" I thawed rapidly and called him.

"I'm sorry I missed your call. What's going on?"

"You couldn't possibly remember your words from four months ago when I lost my job, pastor, could you?"

"Well, let's blame it on my age if I can't, but you obviously do.

What did I say?"

"You said something like, 'The Lord will deliver you from every evil work,' or words to that effect."

"Oh, yeah, Martin. That'd be 2 Timothy 4:18."

"Guess what? I just got a call from a company I applied to a month ago, and they hired me! The paperwork is on its way. I'm the new head of operations for them, and they provide a company car, paid vacation, a pension, health insurance, and lots of other benefits."

"Talk money, Mart."

"It's double what I was earning in the previous job."

. . .

Sunday service had ended well. Our worship had been vibrant, and Sangita took my wife and me to lunch at our favorite bistro. At first I thought the peace in Sangita was due to our service or her satisfaction in the new car she had just purchased, but neither of these added up to the glow I saw on her.

"Is there something you want to tell us?" I asked.

"Hmm, maybe, just maybe, pastor. Why?" she answered, peering at the rearview mirror to glance at me.

"C'mon then. I know I'm right."

"Does 1 Corinthians 10:13 ring any bells with you?"

"Well, it mentions God's faithfulness and escaping temptation."

"Exactly. For you, that may be just another good promise in the Bible, but for Vanya and me, it has become a real-life experience. She was dismissed from the hospital two weeks ago with a clean bill of health and has already resumed her duties at the office a week ago tomorrow."

"Blimey! How in the world did you keep such news to yourself that long? No wonder you are so joyful."

. . .

The atmosphere was electric. The dust hung in the air. Eyes were aglow, brows still wet and sticky with sweat, backs steamy with perspiration. The percussive sound of the native drums rumbled and pulsated through the praise service reminiscent of a tradition that went back to time immemorial. Long-legged dancers sporting bare feet synced their steps to one catchy oldie after another. Some of the African voices that had been roaring out these out-of-tune notes in chorus were now hoarse, but who cared? The adoration was authentic and heartfelt. The Creator is well pleased. A long-anticipated international guest preacher had finally arrived at this remote rural setting.

He was welcomed to the raised reddish mud-brick podium by the resident Pastor who spoke English in a heavy Rwandese accent. He was flanked by a passionate interpreter, clad in starched coffee-colored trousers and his just-about-matching short-sleeved jacket. This combination is indigenously called a Kaunda suit.

I am Brian, Brian MacLaine. I'm eternally grateful to God for counting a former loser like me on His world outreach agenda. Because of His mercies, I've safely arrived in this beautiful part of the world—the first of seven gatherings I will be visiting while I am here.

I was delivered from the grip of hopelessness and drug abuse and came to know the reality of God's love that has been shed abroad in our hearts by the Holy Spirit, according to Romans 5:5. I received Christ in my heart, a call to ministry, and my commission to the nations so that now I have the opportunity to speak into the lives of others with the all-powerful, life-changing Word of God. Much of what we are today can be traced to words—words that have been spoken into our lives. In my case, I received a reassurance a year ago from a servant of God who didn't give up on me, even when my life was on the verge of falling apart.

And so I'd like to reciprocate God's love here today by being a blessing to anyone in this crowd who might be in an awkward place, a painful place, a place that seems insurmountable. Perhaps you've actually given up on yourself. Perhaps you've come to your wit's end and are in a tough time. Let's open our Bibles and read God's Word, beginning with Mark 5:21. . . .

. . .

In each and every case, God stands true to using His Word to encourage, exhort, and edify His people; He is constantly with us and true to His Word.

The Benefits of Reassuring Speech

Reassuring speech rooted in the Word of God attracts angelic assistance in the affairs of man, as angels stand in agreement with the Word of God, which they (the angels) heed (Ps. 103:20).

- Reassuring speech activates the apostolic and priestly ministry of Jesus Christ in our lives. The King James Version says it like this:

  Therefore, holy brethren, partakers of the heavenly calling, consider the Apostle and High Priest of our confession, Christ Jesus.

  —Hebrews 3:1, KJV

- Reassuring speech injects new life into withering and waning faith. Scripture says:

  *Beat your plowshares into swords and your pruning hooks into spears; **let the weak say, "I am strong."***

  —Joel 3:10, emphasis added

CHAPTER 4

RIGHT POSITIONING

You will not need to fight in this battle. **Position yourselves,**
stand still and see the salvation of the Lord, *who is with you, O*
Judah and Jerusalem!

—2 Chronicles 20:17, emphasis added

It matters where you are. Your position is crucial geographically, intellectually, financially, strategically, emotionally, and relationally. At any one point, you are always positioned somehow, without your permission.

It stands to reason, then, that something somewhere in your life must be repositioned when dealing with hard times. We must reposition ourselves if we are to experience change. Every setback is an occasion to rethink our position, an opportunity to rebrand, reinvent, recalibrate, and retool ourselves and rebound! The critically acclaimed Hollywood actor Sylvester Stallone once said: "It ain't about how hard you hit. It's about how hard you can get hit and keep moving on. That's how winning is done."[1]

We are all familiar with the biblical story of the fall of man in Genesis. Our great-great grandparents, whom God placed in a garden perfectly prepared for their enjoyment, messed up big time. Interestingly, the text tells us that when God came by in the cool of the day, the first question He asked them wasn't, "What were you guys thinking trying to be smart with that downer, the devil?" Neither did His question have anything to do with their sin. God's most pressing concern had to do with positioning. His question was, "Adam, where are you?" He was implying that whatever may have transpired could be directly traced to Adam's drift away from the position he was supposed to live in. We can always wreck our lives if we try to function outside of the parameters God has given us. It matters where you are.

In the real estate industry, it is rightly believed that the three factors that impact a property's value most are location, location, and location. The obvious implication in this assertion is that positioning is of such mega importance that it is second to nothing else.

WE WILL ALWAYS WRECK OUR LIVES IF WE FUNCTION OUTSIDE THE PARAMETERS GOD HAS GIVEN US.

Your position determines not only what you experience and how you see, hear, and experience things, but who actually sees, hears, and engages *you* or comes to your aid in the suffering that you experience. Your position determines what you do, the habits you form, the associations you make, and the quality and quantity of fruit you bear. Productivity can be a geographical matter. No, productivity, or the lack of it, *is* a geographical matter.

In the first psalm we read thus:

Blessed is the man who walks not in the counsel of the ungodly, nor stands in the path of sinners, nor sits in the seat of the scornful; but his delight is in the law of the LORD, and in His law he meditates day and night. He shall be like a tree planted by the rivers of water, that brings forth its fruit in its season, whose leaf also shall not wither; and whatever he does shall prosper.

—Psalm 1:1–3

In these verses, the psalmist metaphorically likens a blessed man to a tree planted by rivers of water. Therefore, the timely fruitfulness and the evergreen leaf of this tree can be directly traced to the positioning that the tree enjoys.

PRODUCTIVITY, OR THE LACK OF IT, IS A GEOGRAPHICAL MATTER.

CHAPTER 5

· · · · · · · · · · ·

REMAINING IN PLACE

So Isaac stayed put in Gerar. —Genesis 26:6, MSG

The story is told of a snake that one day made its way into a carpenter's cabin. As the snake stealthily wriggled through an opening in the carpenter's beat up shack, it scraped against some jagged object that it couldn't quite figure out. It quickly turned and ferociously sank its fangs into what turned out to be a saw that the carpenter had stowed in a teeth-up position. Sadly, the snake got severe oral lacerations when it bit into the carpenter's saw. Being vexed about what had happened, the snake took the saw for a vicious attacker and instinctively wrapped itself around this "attacker" with the tightest squeeze it could marshal, so as to wring the living daylights out of its brutal assailant.

Unfortunately, the snake's offensive tactic became the means by which it was shredded into pieces as it constricted itself around the jagged edges of the blade. So tight was the squeeze that the snake eventually bled to death. The poor snake was a victim of its own making.

In a bad situation, it's common for us to make matters worse in our frenzied attempts at saving ourselves when all that is required is to stay put. Sometimes we overreact to the hurt that others have brought to us, and we end up compounding our own pain. It is all too tempting to feel that we must intervene in every adversarial circumstance we encounter. However, there are situations that require mature forbearance instead. Sometimes we should simply ignore an issue, lest we intervene at our own peril.

I couldn't possibly agree more with Ryan Holiday when, elaborating on how to use obstacles against themselves, he writes:

> We wrongly assume that moving forward is the only way to progress, the only way we can win. Sometimes, staying put, going sideways, or moving backward is actually the best way to eliminate what blocks or impedes your path.
>
> There is a certain humility required in the approach. It means accepting that the way you originally wanted to do things is not possible. You just haven't got it in you to do it the "traditional" way. But so what?
>
> What matters is whether a certain approach gets you to where you want to go. And let's be clear, using obstacles against themselves is very different from doing nothing. Passive resistance is, in fact, incredibly active. But those actions come in the form of discipline, self-control, fearlessness, determination, and grand strategy.[1]

Could it be that tough times should be intermissions in which we do not take shortcuts or employ quick fixes, but give God the benefit of the doubt and allow Him to do His work and speak peace to our raging storms instead?

All too often quick-fix heresies promise a life in clover. These quickly find millions of gullible ears—ears that are already itching to hear its false messages. History is full of examples of these people, but even so they should be blamed with moderation and judged with leniency. Here's why: Which one of us would not choose a shot of high living as advocated by the quasi-faith preacher, especially if we've been unwittingly enrolled in the rat race, living in a tenement on Nowhere Street in Stuck-in-the-Mire borough in downtown Frustration City, which is in Broke, Busted, and Disgusted State?

For the soul that has only known sickness for a long time, the quick-fix pseudo-gospel as peddled by the perfect health doctrine is hard to challenge because it gives the hurting a new ecstatic high, a compelling promise they want to believe in. Unfortunately, it leaves no room for endurance and patience—indispensable ingredients in the equation of survival.

But here is the problem: The high that is experienced (if ever) is so short-lived that it leaves its victims in a worse state than it found them in. The hangover in which the hurting writhe in the aftermath of the high is an unwelcome side effect all of us can surely do without. Alex W. Ness wrote:

> Too often the proponents and dispensers of quick cures for spiritual aches and pains become popular and rich through effective merchandising of their teaching but they become victims of their own cures. Because the prescription calls for high living . . . holiness becomes a lost entity. All too often they fall, or are exposed by the ever-searching hungry press, who

gloats to see the downfall of a supposed holiness preacher.[2]

Our Creator says:

> *Be still, and know that I am God; I will be exalted among the nations, I will be exalted in the earth!*
>
> —*Psalm 46:10*

It is a tall order to require us to be still in a chaotic situation by a Deity who lives outside of the limitations that characterize humanity, time, and space. People are naturally averse to situations that strip them of the control they want to command. Hopeless situations, therefore, translate to us as the clearest demonstration of our lack of control, and being the control freaks we all are, we don't like this at all. When we realize that things are out of hand, the natural instinct is to scamper in the face of impending havoc, especially when survival seems unlikely.

Yet God sometimes seems to be saying that you can only ever get to know Him as a strong Refuge and Deliverer when you stay still, regaining your composure and not succumbing to whatever menace the hardships and challenges that riddle your life have brought. This requires real faith.

In Genesis 26, Isaac had every reason to escape to safety, owing to the severity of the famine that had hit the land. For starters, it was the exact example his dad, Abraham, had set in years past when a similar recession had hit the land. In such circumstances, you don't reinvent the wheel. Instead, you follow in the footsteps of your predecessors, such as Abraham, who set the faith bar pretty high.

Secondly, everybody in the area had reacted to the famine by hitting the highway that hopefully led to greener pastures elsewhere. Today we no longer depend on agricultural produce as a means of survival, so the issue of famine could mean little, but for people like Isaac, whose farming was the backbone of his livelihood, this was nothing short of a full-blown recession.

When God appeared to Isaac and instructed him to respond to the famine in terms contrary to Isaac's natural instincts, not only were these instructions against the grain of common sense, but they opened huge questions. The Bible says:

> Then the LORD appeared to him and said: "Do not go down to Egypt; live in the land of which I shall tell you. Dwell in this land, and I will be with you and bless you; for to you and your descendants I give all these lands, and I will perform the oath which I swore to Abraham your father. And I will make your descendants multiply as the stars of heaven; I will give to your descendants all these lands; and in your seed all the nations of the earth shall be blessed.
>
> —Genesis 26:2–4

For the most part, God's instructions often seem opposed to our reality and contrary to our own common sense, but when we gather the courage to heed His bidding and follow His lead, the pieces of the puzzle soon come together and make sense.

It takes courage to obey God. In the words of Plato, the Greek philosopher, "Courage is knowing what not to fear."[3] And so, I say: go ahead and be courageous. Someone once said: "Courage is going from failure to failure without losing enthusiasm."

Planted versus Potted

A few years ago on a cold winter morning, I was returning from a two-week intensive ministry engagement, during which I had traveled from Waltham, Massachusetts, to Silver Spring, Maryland, where (as it turned out) I was to savor the unbridled hospitality and camaraderie of a pastor friend. And oh my, was that a timely and much-needed break!

Finally my childhood dream of visiting the Big Apple also became a reality because getting to Maryland meant that I was to stop over and connect via New York City. As my return flight to London out of Washington's Dulles International Airport in nearby Washington, DC, was a few days away, and my onward journey to Silver Spring could be deferred by a few hours, I thought I'd visit Ground Zero since I was only a few blocks away. And so I did.

As I approached, I was particularly drawn to a twenty-eight-to-thirty-foot tree standing adorned with blue ribbons. Filled with curiosity over the throng of visitors surrounding the tree, I drew closer and was just in time to hear the director of design for the 9/11 memorial site give a narrative that explained the history and uniqueness of this Callery pear tree named Survivor.

Survivor was indeed the eponymous heroine who now lives to tell the story, in pear tree lingo, of what it takes to be a survivor. Having been *planted* near Building 5 of the World Trade Center in the '70s, she had been blooming in natural white as though to bring a touch of life in defiance of her lifeless concrete surroundings ever since. The director said that although Survivor had unfortunately disappeared beneath the fallen towers when the terrorist attacks occurred in 2001, it was uncovered again in the frantic cleanup that ensued the following month. She was smashed, mangled, battered, and pinned between blocks of concrete by the tragic events of that day. They sent Survivor off to the Parks and Recreation Department nursery to see whether anything of its decapitated trunk could be salvaged, and they were overjoyed when Survivor lived up to what was to become her name. A few days later, she was *planted* in rich soil and watered well after her dead tissue had been cut away and her roots trimmed properly.

It quickly became clear to me what the Scripture already quoted was about. To be a survivor, one must commit to remaining put in the hurricanes and tornadoes of adversity that invariably come beating hard against the tapestry of one's faith and aspirations. To survive, you need to have been planted, *not* potted. You want to resonate with the lyrics of the classic and time-honored hymn and say:

My hope is built on nothing less

Than Jesus' blood and righteousness.

I dare not trust the sweetest frame

But wholly trust in Jesus' name.

On Christ the solid rock I stand;

All other ground is sinking sand,

All other ground is sinking sand.[4]

The director speaking in New York City beckoned us to fast forward to the spring of 2010, nine years later, when Survivor encountered another ordeal. It was blown over by a gale. This time its roots were partially exposed, but thanks to the speedy response and relentless work of the Bronx-based Parks and Recreation Department staff, it was hoisted back upright using a heavy-duty crane-equipped truck. Survivor was packed and stuffed with mulch and compost and water-sprayed back to life. Once again, Survivor survived! No wonder it now stands tall, having been incorporated into the memorial design near the base of what was once the South Tower.

There is a conspicuous quality of immovability that comes with being steadfast, standing your ground, remaining put when shaky times make their way toward you. It's easier said than done, but trusting God is a good thing—better than panicking, in any case. The Bible says:

> Those who trust in the LORD are like Mount Zion, which cannot be moved, but abides forever.
>
> —Psalm 125:1

Can you imagine the beauty of being compared to Mount Zion? Can you fathom the power of being as immovable as a mountain that cannot be shaken but abides forever? Imagine standing firm like this mountain no matter what. That is who we are in Christ.

CHAPTER 6

RESETTING PRIORITIES

*But seek first the kingdom of God and His righteousness, and
all these things shall be added to you.*

—Matthew 6:33

Not everything that is urgent is important. Surviving tough times requires that you learn to discern, decipher, and distinguish between the urgent and the truly important because the energy you expend trying to fix the urgent might be better spent fixing the important, which has a direct bearing on your real progress and destiny. Paul knew this all too well when he said:

Therefore I run thus: not with uncertainty. Thus I fight: not as one who beats the air.

—*1 Corinthians 9:26*

He was conscious of the need to target and tackle the real issues of life. He knew that misplaced energy is wasted energy—energy that could have been used to take care of worthwhile causes.

That's why he used the phrase *not as one who beats the air*.

Beating the air saps our resources. Your energy is depleted by beating the air to the same degree it would be if you were actually hitting the right target. What a waste! It is important that we hit the bullseye instead.

Sometimes the most pressing demands on your financial, emotional, mental, and scheduling resources are also the most needlessly distressing. They have nothing to do with the worthwhile matters that lie beneath the surface. These could be projects, problems, phone calls, or people who leave you drained after you've done all you can to help them. The trouble is that it is often hard to tell which is which.

Nowadays folks are masters of disguise. Our planet is devoted to social media, where people constantly change and feign their profiles and even their actual photos so they can appear more compelling than they really are. Folks masquerade as plastic versions of the natural people they ought to be. They wear heavy makeup only because they find masks a bit too much but the lengths to which some go in jazzing up their looks leave the rest of us aghast. It's all just too much.

Our looks-obsessed, sex-crazed world also sports a subculture that religiously advocates for plastic surgery as a remedy over real changes and a healthy lifestyle. It's all about covering up. It is better to look good than to look grisly, but my God! Whatever happened to inner beauty? Since when did the shapes, lips, hips, six-packs, biceps, and triceps take over the world in which modesty, manners, courtesy, honesty, loyalty, respect, and truth used to reign supreme?

Surely it would be remiss of us to hold our peace and twiddle our thumbs while virtues such as faithfulness, love, fairness, and integrity are increasingly marginalized and sometimes sacrificed on the altar of appearances and fame. Sadly, these made-up and mask-wielding souls have made inroads in the pews and pulpits of our places of worship and are now part of the church worldwide. This wouldn't be horrible if these people changed after becoming Christians and joining church families, but many do not.

We are all at liberty to come to Christ just as we are, but we must not stay the same way we came. We need to allow the Holy Spirit the leeway, liberty, and latitude to change our hearts because in Christ we must be transformed and not just reformed—and this, from the inside out. In fact, God promises:

> I will give you a new heart and put a new spirit within you; I will take the heart of stone out of your flesh and give you a heart of flesh.
>
> —Ezekiel 36:26

When Jesus taught that people were to seek first the kingdom of God and His righteousness, He wasn't discounting the need to attend to any other matters. He was simply laying out the correct protocol to follow in our spirituality if we are to attain lasting fulfillment in our lives. He knew that when people struggle to cope with the particularly painful aspects of their living experience, they tend to lean more toward the pressing problems than they do toward the simple solutions. In so doing, fixing the problems becomes the priority. So Jesus was saying that once the priorities are set right, all the other pressing needs we have would, in turn, be addressed as a bonus—an additional benefit to the resolution of the important things that really count. Loosely translated, an African proverb I know says, "The bonus is never slight."

The Wrong Way Around

I remember many years ago when, with keen interest, I watched how the world-famous Mr. Bean (played by Rowan Atkinson) was going to don his swimwear on top of his trousers before taking a dive into the sea. In this episode, the well-dressed Mr. Bean is at the beachfront enjoying a stroll when he fancies a quick swim in the beautiful ocean. He knows he needs to change into swimwear but can't be bothered to go to the changing rooms, which are inconveniently distant from his vantage point at the beach. He figures that he will be able to put his suit on top of his trousers and then work his way out of his clothes without removing the swimwear. He is focused on appearing dressed in front of a nearby gentleman reclining in his folding chair.

MISPLACED ENERGY IS WASTED ENERGY.

In his typical clumsy fashion, he fidgets, jerks, pulls, tugs, and pushes while frequently glancing at the gentleman wearing sunglasses a few yards away. Finally Mr. Bean removes his trousers and proudly walks toward the ocean. As he does, the gentleman rises from his chair and begins to walk away, feeling his way around with a walking stick. It dawns on Mr. Bean that all his hysterical fiddling was needless because the man is blind and wouldn't have seen a pink elephant had Mr. Bean as good as waved it right in front of his nose. There are many possible morals to this story. Here's one: You always get drained much more if you go about things the wrong way around. If you plan to go somewhere, *how* you get there is just as important as getting there.

First Comes First

It is with good reason that commercial airlines have developed first-class travel options. Those who fly first-class have special lounges where they await the boarding call while being entertained with a cornucopia of treats that would instill undiluted jealousy in the hearts of those who fly other classes. While economy passengers wait on hard chairs, first-class passengers are literally a horse of another color, given the hospitality they enjoy. One well-known airline even boasts of providing massages to its first-class passengers to get an edge over its competitors. First-class passengers are given priority before, during, and after the flight. They board first and disembark first. They come first, and it is the *value* and not the *price* of flying first-class that you ought to explore.

Pivotal to surviving tough times is the realization that *priorities must be reset*. If, for example, you own or run a business, are you going to prioritize profits over the people who feed the business with their hard-earned money? Do your financial aspirations come first, or does customer satisfaction take center stage in order to secure consistent repeat business for your enterprise? In your social life, are you going to have friends (who are not part of your family) come first, or family?

Going back to the drawing board and resetting your financial, social, spiritual, health, time management, and career priorities can be the deciding factor to surviving your difficulties. If things are left to find their own balance, your life will probably come to a grinding halt. Leaving things to find their own way when they never have before—expecting a different outcome from the same exact actions that ended badly in the past—has been rightly defined as insanity.

For many people, coming to Christ signals that they have pretty much exhausted all the other options available to them but are still none the wiser regarding their goals. Jesus strikes them as some kind of superman—the quintessential Savior who will fix their issues and help them so they will never have to suffer again. He will solve their dental problems, and their teeth will become porcelain white and squeaky clean ever after. For some, Jesus even possesses incendiary powers. He might send fire from heaven to incinerate their enemies. A life of peace, prosperity, and power is guaranteed!

For students, Jesus will dramatically help their grades go up—transforming any blockheaded simpleton into a gleaming genius! If they are working-class folk, accumulated debt will be magically eradicated, and He will rebuke those weight problems too, probably in King James Version lingo, solemnly declaring, "Woman! Thou art delivered this very hour from this, thine weight."

Max Lucado's sarcasm delivers when he writes:

For some, Jesus is a good luck charm. The "Rabbit's Foot Redeemer." Pocket sized. Handy. Easily packaged. Easily understood. Easily diagrammed. You can put his picture on your wall or you can stick it in your wallet as insurance. You can frame him. Dangle him from your rear-view mirror or glue him to your dashboard. His specialty? Getting you out of a jam. Need a parking place? Rub the redeemer. Need help on a quiz? Pull out the rabbit's foot. No need to have a relationship with him. No need to love him. Just keep him in your pocket next to your four-leaf clover.[1]

Later, as they linger longer with Jesus, it eventually dawns on them (and this could be years later) that the Messiah has His priorities set in a hierarchy totally dissonant to theirs. His priorities are the polar opposite of theirs. Their fantasy of a life of total bliss disintegrates right under their noses. They discover that they need to be made more like Jesus. It is not part of Jesus' plan to change for them. He is most definitely not interested in being changed to suit them. They are the ones who must be changed. They learn that canceling their debts without learning how not to incur them in the first place is the same as fetching water in a basket with holes in it from a distant well.

Instead of magically helping their grades go up, they realize that Jesus graces them with His presence as they burn the midnight oil. They are learning discipline. They are beginning to see the correct order of Jesus' workings in their lives. It is now becoming clear why the kingdom and God's righteousness come first. They see that all the rest trails behind as bonuses. They understand that if they are to survive their tough times, they must reset their priorities.

CHAPTER 7

RISING PATIENTLY

Therefore humble yourselves under the mighty hand of God,
that He may exalt you in due time.

—1 Peter 5:6, emphasis added

In Christ, the way up is down. Oxymoronic? Maybe. But stay the course, and you'll soon catch my drift.

Many times when God sets His eye on a better future for you (which He perpetually does), He allows adversity to temporarily weigh you down. Your most ardent prayers seem to fall on deaf ears, and your hope for relief hurls you downward rapidly. There seems to be this severe disconnect from God and it feels like the peace that you previously enjoyed has long evaporated. You become restless. Your spirits are low. You are downcast, and you feel vulnerable and frustrated because nothing seems to be moving the way you think it ought to move. You can't see a way out of your misery, so stress sets in.

If this miserable situation is prolonged, your stress turns chronic. Instead of seeing that you have a glass with something in it, all you see is the fact that it is half empty. No wonder, then, that in the UK alone, it is now estimated that nine out of every ten people who visit the doctor have problems related to stress. That is staggering! However, this horrid situation can be a good thing. Why? Your mind becomes open and pliable in these circumstances. Your latent creativity is stirred as you begin to figure out the ways and means of surviving. It is time to separate what works from what doesn't. And this is important.

The Old Testament prophet Jeremiah found himself in such a place. Feeling a touch hard-pressed, he asked God questions that he wouldn't have asked had his situation not deteriorated to such a place. He asked:

> *Why is my pain perpetual and my wound incurable, which refuses to be healed? Will You surely be to me like an unreliable stream, as waters that fail?*
>
> *—Jeremiah 15:18*

God responded, saying:

> *"If you return, then I will bring you back; you shall stand before Me; **if you take out the precious from the vile, you shall be as My mouth.**"*
>
> *—Jeremiah 15:19, emphasis added*

For the duration of your tough time, you need to separate the vile from the valuable. These could by turns be principles, places, people, or philosophies. You must recalibrate, reroute, refocus, reflect on, and revisit ideologies, relationships, and methodologies that you probably wouldn't have looked at if things had gone your way. This can only be a good thing.

It is time to unlearn the wrong stuff that you learned and learn the good stuff that you should have learned and practiced long before the onset of your plight. It is possible that you could have avoided your pain had you been a disciplined and consistent doer of the good stuff in the first place. The psalmist speaks to God, saying:

> It is good for me that I have been afflicted, that I may learn Your statutes.
>
> —Psalm 119:71

There are many people who see learning as a menace because it involves demolishing some sacred cows and discarding cherished ways of going about life, regardless of their flaws and attending collateral damage. It is far better to re-examine our lives and habits and learn, gaining fresh insights that will serve God and grant us peace.

Talking about learning in his book titled *People Skills*, Neil Thompson notes that:

It is also often the case that an acceptance of learning is seen as a sign of weakness, an acknowledgment that there is a deficit that needs to be made up. This negative and defensive view of learning is an unnecessary barrier to . . . development, and could so easily pave the way for a form of routinized, uncritical practice.[1]

There are some things you will only learn about yourself and others when you are at an all-time low—a trial in your life. If you have not developed the kind of humility necessary to sustain you in a high position, it is hard to exhibit. The psalmist articulated the correct sequence when he wrote:

> Before destruction the heart of a man is haughty, and before honor is humility.

> —Proverbs 18:12

There is a sizable degree of character that we only develop when we are slowed down and stopped in our tracks. You need to develop character and fortitude *before* you are catapulted into a realm that requires it even more. Thomas Paine, the English-born American political activist of the late eighteenth century is quoted as once saying, "Reputation is what men and women think of us; character is what God and angels know of us."[2]

This goes against the grain of the route most people would rather take in scaling the ladder of success, but I have been around long enough to observe that it still is the way to go as far as God is concerned.

St. Augustine is quoted as having once said:

"Do you wish to rise?

Begin by descending.

You plan a tower that will pierce the clouds?

Lay first the foundation of humility."[3]

Although God's ultimate goal in dealing with us is to lift us up, it is important to understand that He will quite often approach this from an angle that is diametrically opposed to the way we would rather do it. If you want to make it through tough times when you hit them (and you will), you need to know the following:

- No tough times last forever. They can only go on for so long. The psalmist articulates this very ably:

    Weeping may endure for a night, but joy comes in the morning.

    —Psalm 30:5

In other words, unbeknownst to you, your tough times could very well be easing off, even right now as you read this. The three-dimensional world in which we live often takes time to catch up with the reality that has already happened in the spirit realm. Should you hang in there long enough, your morning is sure to bring with it this joy unspeakable, full of glory! Make no mistake about it, joy is coming in the morning. The difference between *mourning* and *morning* is *u*.

- Every strangling point in your pilgrimage has an expiration date; it is just invisible to the naked eye. Trials are "working" within a time frame in a time-sensitive manner. The Bible settles this further when it says:

    *But may the God of all grace, who called us to His eternal glory by Christ Jesus, **after you have suffered a while**, perfect, establish, strengthen, and settle you.*

    —1 Peter 5:10, emphasis added

Notice that the perfection, establishment, strengthening, and settlement come into the equation *after* you have suffered a while. Meanwhile, there is hope that your deliverance is on the way. You are that much closer to the end of your trouble, not any further away.

- Everybody encounters a tough time at some point in his or her life. Therefore, your survival through it depends heavily on your understanding of the fact that you are not unique in suffering through one.

  *No temptation has overtaken you except such as is **common to man**.*

  —*1 Corinthians 10:13, emphasis added*

- Hardship is not a strange occurrence. We live in a fallen world, so there will be frequent mishaps, dilemmas, suffering, inexplicable pain, dysfunction, injustice, and unfairness. We learn about this from the Bible too.

  Beloved, do not think it strange concerning the fiery trial which is to try you, as though some strange thing happened to you.

  —*1 Peter 4:12*

- Scripture says that God Himself (not any of the angels) resists the proud but exalts the humble (1 Pet. 5:5). It is a horrible thing to be resisted by God. To whom do you run when it dawns on you that you are being resisted by the Creator? Where do you lodge a complaint against the Almighty? Who arbitrates in your favor when you are at odds with God? Which attorney can litigate against an omniscient, omnipresent, and omnipotent Deity? So if you are being humiliated and humbled by a trial, take solace in the fact that you will in due season be exalted.

- Every tough time comes with its own built-in solution.

*No temptation has overtaken you except such as is common to man; but God is faithful, who will not allow you to be tempted beyond what you are able, **but with the temptation will also make the way of escape, that you may be able to bear it.***

—*1 Corinthians 10:13, emphasis added*

I was peasant African, born and bred. My culture had an eccentric affinity with time. Back there, time wasn't supposed to be measured in seconds, minutes, and hours. Neither were the wages of workers and laborers structured around hours. A day was sunrise to sunset. Dawn and dusk were the benchmarks. Most food was covered, wrapped up even, and slow cooked, if for nothing else but to keep its delicate aroma around until dinnertime. Mealtimes were not so much about fending off hunger as they were a social ceremony. Somehow folks knew how to do business while eluding busyness. They had time.

I think that was a great way to take many of the irritating details of each day out of the way and swap them with a more whole and broader view for each day. Those folks knew how to elude micromanaging and leaned more toward mastering the bigger picture. This required a laid-back, patient approach to living.

Against that backdrop, I would offer this counsel: Season the steak of your story with tons of the salt of patience. The glory that emanates from your story will be tastier. Rise patiently. Run your own race. Shun the shallowness of competitive jealousy. You will survive. The all-time great philosopher Aristotle once said, "Patience is bitter, but its fruit is sweet."[4]

CHAPTER 8

RIGHTFUL PARTNERSHIP

*So they signaled to their **partners in the other boat** to come
and help them. And they came and filled both the boats, so
that they began to sink.*

—Luke 5:7, emphasis added

The rich and famous that we tend to envy and idolize are
many. Ranging from professional sports personalities to movie
celebrities, business moguls to political activists, singers to
software billionaires, all have one thing in common: they didn't
ever make it alone. The legendary athlete Michael Jordan once
said, "Talent wins games, but teamwork and intelligence wins
championships."[1]

There isn't very much you can achieve by yourself. You are not
wired to be a Lone Ranger in life. With regard to the reality that
people can be difficult, teamwork still remains the name of the
game. Could it be that you are right in the middle of a trial because
you have been toughing it out solo? Writes Mike Williams:

Very few accomplishments of major proportion happen without the support of trusted family members, colleagues, or friends. They are the key figures in your base of support. The reality of moving through tough times is that the input of a trusted group of people can be invaluable in weighing options and priorities, making good decisions, creating key inroads, and evaluating your progress at critical stages.[2]

In discussing the process of continually evaluating and upgrading your skill or talent level, he further notes that:

The real thing to know about your talent or skill is that you need people around you who can help evaluate your status and progress, so that ultimately you meet the standard that allows you to present and represent your stuff.[3]

From the very beginning, when God's seven-day creation extravaganza drew to a close, He noted, probably with grave concern, that the first man, Adam, was in a lonely place. You can be lonely even in a crowd. For the first time in the creation story, God verbalized His displeasure with that situation, saying, "It is not good" (Gen. 2:18).

God's displeasure was caused by the fact that Adam had no human partner suitable for Him. We all know that God embarked on creating a rightful partner for the man, and the rest is history.

God uses our time, talent, and treasure. You need God, and you need others in order to survive any tough times in your life. There isn't a whole lot you can do without God. By the same token, there really isn't a lot that God will do without you, even though He could if He wanted. *Partnership is the name of the game.* Partnership with God and other people is required to handle the bite of being in a tight and painful place.

A wrench that often fouls up a partnership is pride. Pride is a distorted view of reality. It is a twisted assessment of one's potential. Pride often says, "I'm OK. I can do without God. I'm big and bold enough to make it through without anyone's assistance. I don't really need help. I will tough it out by myself." And so it goes on and on. In the meantime, all hope of surviving our trials dwindles, much to the pleasure of the enemy of our souls, the devil.

It is interesting to note that in pretty much all His dealings with mankind, the all-knowing, self-sufficient, almighty God, in His matchless and sovereign wisdom, chooses partnership over patronization as the more prudent route. Just before He destroyed the ancient cities of Sodom and Gomorrah, He sought the intercessory mediation of the patriarch, Abraham. The forgiving and tender-hearted side of His character partnered with this elderly man so that the impending judgment and attending retribution could be averted.

The thing is that if God can find a man with whom He can partner in your neighborhood, village, city, community, or nation, He can relent from executing judgment because of His relationship with that one person. The question is, can you be that rightful partner?

Partnership is critical in turning the tide in times of distress, desperation, and despondency. In fact, it is the game changer when seasons of shortage, lack, and uncertainty are the order of the day. *God's Little Devotional Book II* says:

> *One of the great lessons of experience is when we learn that we are not the prime motivator or catalyst of the success we experience in life. While we may be the engineer of our own failures more often than we care to admit, we rarely reach the heights of success on our own. We always have the help of others in reaching the top—regardless of our field or endeavor—and ultimately we are enabled by God. We accomplish only what He enables us to.[4]*

The opening scriptural text of this chapter clearly teaches us this one thing: that by having rightful partnership with others, our capacity to achieve and our productivity in the workplace are exponentially multiplied. As long as Simon Peter went solo in terms of raking in the catch, he was always going to really struggle with handling the miracle that had just been placed in his reach. It took the cooperation and partnership of other men in another boat to manage the amazing provision orchestrated by the creative utterance of Jesus as He stood by the lake that day.

Anomalous Arithmetic

In Leviticus 26, we are introduced to an anomalous code of arithmetic. This is a perfect example of the power of rightful partnership, when God spells out the blessings that ought to attend our living experience when we walk in His statutes and keep His commandments. He says:

Five of you shall chase a hundred, and a hundred of you shall put ten thousand to flight; your enemies shall fall by the sword before you.

—Leviticus 26:8

Now, if I get my sums wrong, please blame my eldest son, who was a math major at university at the writing of this and who corroborated my calculations. Besides, math wasn't my strongest subject growing up, anyway, but the above verse would seem to suggest that your productivity is exponentially multiplied whenever you become part of a team, and here's why: If it takes five men to put one hundred enemies to flight, it would logically follow that it takes five hundred men to put ten thousand enemies to flight. However, in this verse, we see that the ten thousand enemies are put to flight by a hundred. In other words, the results achieved by five hundred men are absolutely amazing because they are accomplished by only one hundred. The effectiveness of each of the one hundred men is multiplied fivefold, simply because they each become part of a team and forge a partnership. How good is that!

In Deuteronomy 32, we are once again treated to God's astounding arithmetic by which He enabled the Israelites to conquer their adversaries.

How could one chase a thousand, and two put ten thousand to flight, unless their Rock had sold them, and the Lord had surrendered them?

—Deuteronomy 32:30

Again, we see that one man was able to singlehandedly

fend off a thousand enemies. However, once he became part of a two-man squad, his prowess was exponentially multiplied fivefold. Here's how: If it takes one man to put one thousand enemies to flight, it would follow logically that it takes ten men to put ten thousand enemies to flight. However, in this verse, ten thousand enemies are put to flight by a two-man squad. In other words, the results achieved by ten men are amazingly accomplished by only two! This tells me that the effectiveness of each of the two men is multiplied fivefold by teamwork. How wonderful.

Against All Odds

A bronze statue of author, lecturer, and political activist Helen Keller stands in the collection of the National Statuary Hall in Washington, DC.[5] Born in West Tuscumbia, Alabama, Helen once said: "Alone we can do so little; together we can do so much."

As a woman beset by blindness and deafness at an early age, Helen's statement makes sense. Her trouble began when she was only nineteen months old and she contracted a condition that the doctors described as an "acute congestion of the stomach and brain," which could very well have been scarlet fever or meningitis.[6] It left her deaf and blind.

Against all odds, she developed a gestural communication system that boasted a good sixty home signs by which she could communicate with her family by the time she was seven. Unabridged by her handicap, Helen made her way through her education starting at Perkins Institute for the Blind in May 1888 and eventually became proficient in braille and sign language. She even learned to speak and began giving lectures. Graduating at the age of twenty-four from the Radcliffe College of Harvard University, she became the first deaf-blind person to earn a Bachelor of Arts degree.

How was Helen Keller able to plow through the odds that were stacked up against her from the cradle to the grave? How did she survive through a series of strokes beginning in 1961 all the way to June of 1968 when she died in her sleep at her home? How did Helen earn one of America's highest civilian honors, the Presidential Medal of Freedom, from President Lyndon B. Johnson?[7] How did a braille-using deaf-blind woman who had to have speech therapy so her voice could be heard better by the public become a trailblazing world-famous speaker and author of no fewer than twelve published books and several articles?

The answer lies in the rightful partnerships that characterized her life. For starters, she was deeply spiritual. She knew God. Before she became a Christian, she had said of Jesus Christ, "I always knew He was there, but I didn't know His name!"[8]

Throughout her life, she partnered with an array of wonderful people who helped and supported her, including her lifelong companion and private secretary, Anne Sullivan, who was also visually impaired; Polly Thomson, her Scottish housekeeper; and Winnie Corbally, her nurse. Helen was also friends with many key figures and influential personalities, such as the Scottish-born scientist and inventor Alexander Graham Bell, Mark Twain, Charlie Chaplin, and every American president from Grover Cleveland to Lyndon B Johnson.[9]

CHAPTER 9

· · · · · · · · · · ·

RESOLUTE PURPOSE

For this purpose the Son of God was manifested, that He might destroy the works of the devil.

—1 John 3:8

People who survive difficult trials typically have one trait in common: they share resolute purpose. They assume a mental posture that asserts: *I will not be distracted, discouraged, or disenfranchised. I might take a licking along the way, but boy am I going to keep on ticking! If I get a bunch of lemons, I am gonna make lemonade! I won't be sidetracked, maligned, or confounded. Neither will I sit around trying to make heads or tails about why life often sucks. I am focused on the assignment I carry and committed to the fulfillment of my godly dreams. Anything that does not contribute to my purpose compromises it, and I will not allow anything to do that.* It is no wonder that such people have success in the end.

In defining *purpose*, Brian Tracy writes:

> *This is the one goal that is more important to you than any*

other single goal. It is the one goal that can help you more to achieve more of your other goals than any single achievement.[1]

When Jesus first began His public ministry in Nazareth, He made it a point to clearly define His purpose in His debut public appearance. He authenticated His gracious words by referring to the Word of God, which had predicted His coming centuries earlier. (See Luke 4:17–21.) His resolute purpose was the common thread that ran through His entire ministry. It was to become His hallmark with the Jewish people of His day and remains the same to us who come to faith in God through the legacy of His matchless ministry.

As He neared the conclusion of His ministry on earth, it was evident that Jesus had neither strayed from His purpose nor shied away from the high calling on His life. His entire ministry was strewn with hostility from religious folk, hatred from people in many business quarters, and suspicion from political stakeholders whose leadership ideas stood in stark contrast to the message He preached.

Whether we are to attain to even a fraction of His accomplishments is an entirely different kettle of fish, but the Bible does urge us to follow in His footsteps. Jesus Himself dared us to do greater works than those that He did (John 14:12). So how did Jesus make it through all the trouble He endured? Jesus was so filled with purpose that He always bounced back into action. He only rested on His laurels after the assignment had been accomplished, never beforehand. This enabled Him to get through the worst of the worst.

In her compelling treatise *The Overload Solution,* Jane Alexander writes:

> *Behind all the glitter and gloss of modern life hides a small, unpretentious yet vital task. Your purpose as a human being is to discover your true Self, to find the meaning for your individual life. You need to get in touch with the Self that lies beyond the ego, your true inner Self that is wise, and loving, and balanced, and unique. Finding your true Self is tough hard soul work. You're unlikely to discover it at some weekend workshop; it won't jump out at you when you're lying on your Gucci yoga mat; it won't magically appear if you tie a piece of red string around your wrist. There is no quick-fix method to discover your soul. It's tough work, every-day work. You have to keep questioning yourself, asking, "What is the actual meaning of my life?"*[2]

The Deadly Trio

There is a deadly trio of factors that typically erode many people's resolve to be purposeful in life. This trio is composed of delay, distraction, and diversion. Let's dig a little deeper.

Delay. We live in a fast-paced, deadline-driven world in which any kind of delay is met with animosity. Some people are ridiculously aggressive under the slightest provocation. And yet deadlines per se are not bad. They are necessary parameters that can ignite productivity and reinforce progress. Psychologist, author, and life coach Dr. Rob Yeung writes:

Deadlines are motivating. If you make a promise that you'll do something by a certain date, that's a much bigger commitment than saying "you'll get round to it." A deadline acts as a powerful reminder, a mental kick in the backside.[3]

So it's just that we really loathe delay, and this hatred is pretty understandable because for many individuals and businesses alike, even a little delay makes everything more difficult. Delay can easily translate into severe financial penalties or terrific financial setbacks.

However, delayed pay checks, trains, flights, mail, packages, and expectations are good examples of realities that are the order of the day—instances we must learn to live with. Delay is not denial.

Distraction. A distraction breaks our focus. Distractions often cause people to never realize their dreams. Quoting his mentor, the world-class life coach and motivational speaker Bob Proctor once said, "We are only limited by weakness of attention and poverty of imagination."[4]

Remember that dreams are mental pictures. This is why even in the literal sense pictures that are out of focus are often discarded. Distractions can be things or activities, but most are people. I mean this in the literal sense. We must realize that the biggest problem we face is embracing the wrong people in life.

Clutter is part and parcel of distractions. It is a healthy practice to routinely unclutter your life. When life is cluttered, most people mentally retreat to, and begin to live out of, the least cluttered spot. Priorities change. Life is funneled down Relegation Avenue. Under the spell of a distraction, the inferior, marginal, or secondary gets foisted upon that which is truly important to devastating effect.

Many a vision is rendered ineffective or defunct, thanks to the inner workings and quirks made by distractions whenever these are allowed to hold sway. Could this be the reason that Paul unequivocally declared this to the Corinthian church: "For I determined not to know anything among you except Jesus Christ and Him crucified" (1 Cor. 2:2)?

Diversion. A diversion is a detour. It is a deviation from the direct route to a desired destination. In most instances, it neither directly impedes nor hampers one's progression toward a desired end, but it does take the long way around, and many times too. By the time people note the detour, they may come to the conclusion that theirs are hapless, if not hopeless, endeavors. Discouragement sets in as time is lost, resources are depleted, raw nerves are exposed, and patience and positive results seem distant and hard to find.

WE MUST REALIZE THAT THE BIGGEST PROBLEM WE FACE IS EMBRACING THE WRONG PEOPLE IN LIFE.

For this reason, anyone who even remotely desires to be a person of resolute purpose must be wary of anything that attempts to divert him or her from that purpose.

CHAPTER 10

· · · · · · · · · · ·

RESOUNDING PRAISE

*But at midnight Paul and Silas were praying and singing hymns to God, and the prisoners were listening to them. Suddenly there was a great earthquake, so that the foundations of the prison were shaken; and **immediately all the doors were opened and everyone's chains were loosed.***

—Acts 16:25–26, emphasis added

Something happens when our high praises ascend and are found acceptable to God. I use the word *acceptable* deliberately and carefully because, from a biblical standpoint, not all that passes for praise and worship nowadays is acceptable before God. As in all things required of us from God, our praise must meet His stringent standards and His clear criteria; it must dovetail with the precise parameters clearly articulated in the Bible.

Jesus taught that our worship must be authentic and must emanate from a deep place of spirituality in our hearts. We read this in the Gospel of John:

*But a time is coming and is already here when the true (genuine) worshipers will worship the Father **in spirit** [from the heart, the inner self] **and in truth** (reality); for the Father seeks such people to be His worshipers. God is spirit [the Source of life, yet invisible to mankind], and those who worship Him **must worship in spirit and truth (reality).***

—John 4:23–24, AMP, emphasis and parenthetical text added

Something always capitulates when we ascribe greatness to God in spite of our bondage or pain. I think of this as a divine transaction in which an exchange takes place. When your praise ascends to God, His provision descends to you. When your praise ascends to God, His strength and power descend in exchange.

King David was a great musician and spoke with a considerable measure of authority when he said to God:

But You are holy, enthroned in the praises of Israel.

—Psalm 22:3

In the spirit realm, resounding praise creates a structure from which God begins to exercise dominion over the circumstances that hold us back in the natural realm. One definition of *throne* at Dictionary.com is "the office or dignity of a sovereign."[1] This definition resonates with the thought that resounding praise activates the dignity and sovereignty of God so that His liberating power is released on the issues we are experiencing here on earth.

I honestly believe that the praise and worship you offer up to God in the thick of pain and hardship is more sweet smelling to Him than the kind that you offer up in the aftermath of a favorable development in your life. Painful praise and worship is authentic, and you only function with authority in an area in which you're authentic.

In heaven there are no hardships, no troubles, no bad days, mood swings, hospital admissions, diseases, cases of poverty, pains, job layoffs, or anything negative. Additionally, there are hosts of different angelic beings and heavenly creatures whose sole job is to constantly adore, worship, and praise God.

However, their unending praise offering does not stem from a place of pain in any way, so theirs is not a sacrificial offering. They are not singing the praises of God at the cost of anything else they'd rather be doing. Therefore, the adoration and praise we lavish upon God from our low estate here is more sweet smelling because it comes from a place of sacrifice and brokenness.

Being the free moral agents that we are, we could easily exercise our right to not worship, but the point is that when we worship God, it is because we have chosen to do so amid the diversity of other activities available to us. In heaven there is no other option. The repercussions that promptly attended Lucifer when he rebelled are fresh in the minds of heaven's residents. They would rather enjoy God's presence than do that.

Not There Yet, but Not Back There Either

In the scriptural passage under consideration at the beginning of this chapter, we visited Paul and Silas in jail. It was at midnight that their breakthrough came, and that is noteworthy because midnight is a transitory moment. It is dark. The old day expires and turns into a new one. At midnight, you are detaching yourself from the past but have not fully embraced the present. You have set out from where you've always been but haven't arrived at your destination. You are not there yet, but you are not back there either. You are in *transition*.

YOU ONLY FUNCTION WITH AUTHORITY IN AN AREA WHERE YOU ARE AUTHENTIC.

For Paul and Silas, however, the best way to end a bad day was to engage in a resounding praise party. Similarly, the best way to welcome a new day is to worship God and engage heaven in prayer.

The term *transition* comes into its own in the art of cinematography and video editing. Transitions take place when a sequence of images from one feed is phased out and replaced by another, perhaps from a different feed. This is often achieved with special effects. Particularly notable is the transition effect that introduces a new sequence of images while the images of the preceding sequence are still visible on the monitor and are only faded out over a few seconds when the new sequence is firmly prominent. So the transition is a moment that simultaneously depicts old and new images in the same frames.

Amid the throes of transition, you catch glimpses of where you are headed, which is how you gather the motivation to keep pressing on even though you are still gripped by your current trial.

You get snapshots and sneak previews of what is likely to happen but still remain trapped in the muck of the nasty experience where you actually are. Transitions are by nature precarious. You are neutral and may possibly strike people as noncommittal. However, transitions are by definition exactly that: transitory.

Transition is a watershed moment. Surviving through a transitory season requires that you first and foremost understand what is happening, lest you needlessly deplete your energy in combatting a fleeting situation. If you are in some kind of transition as you read this, hold on and hold tight. Nothing oppressive goes on forever. No tyrant reigns eternally.

Secondly, you need to accept transition and take it for what it is: an ill-defined situation that simultaneously fronts characteristics of two different, and often contradictory, realities. Thirdly, you must maintain your focus on your goals. Do not allow transition the privilege of distracting you from that which matters. Hold your nerve through to the end.

The psalmist said:

> I will bless the LORD at all times; His praise shall continually be in my mouth.

> —Psalm 34:1

These are not the words of someone who was inexperienced in handling adversity. These are the words of a man whose worship was independent of his past, detached from his emotional state. Pleasure, pain, or suffering did not determine his worship. Notice that the psalmist took an all-encompassing stance on the times of offering praise to God. He blessed the Lord at *all times*: the good, the bad, and everything in between. He did this *continually*. God's resounding praises were constantly and incessantly in his mouth. This is what it takes to survive tough times.

In Everything, Not *for* Everything

Entrenched deep within the doctrines and dogma of many religious ideologies is the belief that our fate—hook, line, sinker, the fisherman, and his boots—is entirely in the hands, and within the perfect will, of our Maker. This firmly embraced view has found sympathy in the core belief systems of some of those who subscribe to the teachings of the Bible and confess themselves followers of Christ.

While this position seems plausible, considering the attributes that God is omniscient, omnipresent, and omnipotent, it does not accurately represent what the Bible actually says about us.

> *Rejoice always, pray without ceasing,* **in everything give thanks;** *for this is the will of God in Christ Jesus for you.*
>
> —*1 Thessalonians 5:16–18, emphasis added*

Thanking God *in* everything is light years away from thanking God *for* everything. The former is the balanced biblical position corroborated by the whole counsel of God. The latter is not the same, but a commonplace practice espoused as God's counsel.

Having said that, it must be made crystal clear that it is a scripturally recommended, good, and godly practice, to thank God for the innumerable great things He does for us. I wish time and space allowed me to catalog the many references that validate this.

What, then, is the will of God in Christ Jesus for you? That's an easy one. *Rejoicing always* is the will of God. *Praying without ceasing* is the will of God. *Maintaining a thankful heart* in spite of life's circumstances is the will of God. Listen, we do not thank God for the loss of loved ones when they finally lose their long battle with cancer or AIDS. We simply maintain our posture of gratitude to God in the maladies that crowd our lives, making them anything but perfect. This is not an easy feat either. However, giving thanks in everything is an example of offering resounding praise to God in spite of our current hardship or suffering. It is part of our unconditional worship.

When you are demoted or laid off, you don't thank God for this negative development, but you do stay thankful in your attitude toward Him amid the fray. As the lyrics of the time-honored hymn composed by Johnson Oatman Jr. in 1897 state, you "count your blessings" and "name them one by one." Max Lucado writes, "When you are given an ice cream sundae, you don't complain over a missing cherry."[2]

Science on Side

Since gratitude is a relatively new field in scientific study, researchers are still trying to demystify its cause-and-effect relationship with health benefits. However, recent findings show that thoughts of gratitude actually boost your mood and have other positive effects on your health.

In her article "The Power of Gratitude," Lisa Fields quotes Professor Willibald Ruch of the University of Zurich as saying:

We know from studies that gratitude really does have an impact on happiness, that it increases life satisfaction. . . . It's among the top five predictors of happiness. . . . Nowadays, too many people don't stop to appreciate what they have, much less express gratitude. Our instant-gratification lifestyle may be to blame.[3]

In writing about the long-lasting positive effects of gratitude, Lisa Fields notes that Canadian researchers have found that people who write letters of thanks or perform good deeds like those who participated in a pilot project they undertook, which spanned a mere six-week period, are able to improve their mental health, decrease their bodily pain, feel more energetic, and accomplish more daily tasks.

Swedish researchers have discovered that people age 77 to 90 who are thankful for what they have are less likely to dwell on the chance that they may grow frail.

In the same article, Helena Hörder, a researcher at the University of Gothenburg, is quoted:

When they can't change something, they choose gratitude and focus on what's good: walking on their own legs, still being alive and living by themselves... Maybe it's some kind of confidence that you can cope with this and focus on the right things.[4]

In writing about the need for gratitude, Max Lucado is spot-on when he writes thus:

"You cry over spilled champagne."

Ouch.

Your complaints are not over the lack of necessities but the abundance of benefits. You bellyache over the frills, not the basics; over benefits, not essentials. The source of your problems is your blessings. . . .

Gratitude. More aware of what you have than what you don't. Recognizing the treasure in the simple—a child's hug, fertile soil, a golden sunset. Relishing in the comfort of the common—a warm bed, a hot meal, a clean shirt.[5]

CHAPTER 11

· · · · · · · · · · ·

RAW PASSION

As yet I am as strong this day as on the day that Moses sent me; just as my strength was then, so now is my strength for war, both for going out and for coming in.

—Joshua 14:11

Here is an anecdotal story told of a man who lost family and all he had to the tsunami and Fukushima nuclear plant disaster of March 11, 2011, in Japan. The man responded to a TV crew member's question about whether he had any hope left to live. He turned and pointed to a cherry tree beginning to bloom and said, "Look there, that's what gives me hope." The crew gazed in amazement at the vibrancy and raw passion to live this victim continued to brandish.

What do you do when you wake up one morning and realize you have gone astray, have not reached your dreams, and are behind on your bills? How do you keep your cool when your world is mangled and messy, filled with fright, characterized by chaos, and riddled with rejection? Sucking your thumb while curled up in a fetal position is certainly not an option.

How do you pave your way into a supposedly brighter future against a backdrop of pain and failure? How do you circumnavigate your way around your present when you are living on a shoestring, your credit has gone to the dogs, and your supposed best friends have left you high and dry? Exactly how do you respond to the trials that doggedly seek to imprison your hopes while brazenly flaunting your flaws and failings to everyone in sight?

I have heard that yesterday is in the tomb and tomorrow is in the womb, and all we actually have is today. This may be true, but for the poor souls struggling today in a painful trial, it brings little hope. What must happen today to deliver them from their plight and bring them freedom once again?

There must be a way out, and I'm glad there is, or God wouldn't have promised so. There is hope for the hopeless, health for the unhealthy, and a Father for the fatherless. There are good tidings for the poor, healing for the broken-hearted, liberty for the captives, the opening of prison doors for the bound, and an acceptable year and a day of the vengeance of our God. There is comfort and consolation for those who mourn, beauty for ashes, the oil of joy for mourning, and a garment of praise for the spirit of heaviness. (See Isa. 61:1–3.)

When Jesus said, "Come to Me, all you who labor and are heavy laden, and I will give you rest" (Matt. 11:28), He was demonstrating that God literally calls all people out of trouble into a place of refuge, His lap of recess and restfulness. God knows that life can sometimes hand us such trouble, terror, and trauma that the tally of victims can quickly become insurmountable if, in the nick of time, divine intervention doesn't pull a rabbit out of the hat. That is why He reaches out to the many that are bruised, battered, broken, burned-out, and burdened.

Note that He never beckons people to jump out of the frying pan into the fire. He is a loving, caring, and concerned heavenly Father. And I say this with due sensitivity to the suffering of many people I know personally, who through no fault of their own have had to battle awful circumstances, including complex medical conditions, grief, and loss. God is very familiar with the suffering and hardship with which ordinary regular folks grapple on a daily basis. Speaking of Jesus, the Scripture says:

> *For we do not have a High Priest who cannot sympathize with our weaknesses, **but was in all points tempted as we are, yet without sin.***
>
> —*Hebrews 4:15, emphasis added*

Jesus knew that people don't get weary without cause. Something, or, God forbid, someone, always brings about the kind of rigor necessary to make us weary. He was aware of the burnout that stems from endlessly fighting for ideals, faith, family, friends, finances, and a fairer future. He was saying that no matter how hard life gets or how bad your past may have been, there still remains a future worth waiting for.

God knows that regardless of the many challenges cancerously eating away at you from within and without, you deserve better. His passion for the broken and beleaguered never fails.

Dictionary.com defines *passion* as "any powerful or compelling emotion or feeling, as love or hate." It also defines it as a "strong amorous feeling or desire; love; ardor."[1] Interestingly, the medieval Latin origin of the word springs from the word used specifically to describe Christ's sufferings on the cross, and it cites its many biblical accounts as the best example of passion.[1] I couldn't possibly argue with that. Neither could actor, movie director, scriptwriter, and producer Mel Gibson, who cowrote, produced, and directed a film about Jesus' last days and appropriately christened it *The Passion of the Christ*.[2]

Christ fully models the kind of raw passion we ought to possess if we, like Him, are to endure trials. Surviving tough times depends on your possession of a raw passion for the future you envision. That passion must dwarf your current predicament well enough for you to keep on keeping on.

Hopeless people are difficult to be with, let alone encourage. When decent folks lose hope, moral decay and apathy can follow. Gang culture and the criminal underworld that have mushroomed and thrive in the more deprived neighborhoods of many of the world's inner cities are fueled by hopelessness and a lack of purpose. Gang culture makes up for the sense of belonging and control that its adherents desperately seek but lack because of their situation.

It doesn't matter how voluptuous a woman is or how well-defined a man's muscles are if they remain apathetic about a brighter future. These physical attributes offer a flimsy consolation at best or count for nothing because apathy is the ultimate nemesis of modern life.

Pat Mesiti writes:

Apathy is one of the greatest killers of success. It kills motivation, vision, and destiny. Apathy has to be the ugliest word in the English language. Apathetic people make excuses. They reason away why they are not getting ahead in life or achieving. One common excuse is that they are waiting for the "big break," when all circumstances will be perfect. The reality is, if you're asleep to opportunities, you'll miss all the breaks that come your way.[2]

Life ought to be fun. There is every reason for you to pursue a fulfilling life to the degree that you are connected to, and healthily relate with, God, life's Author. Like my eldest daughter would say as a fledgling teenage entrepreneur, "There are places to go, people to meet, and things to do." While I wondered where she heard that, I agreed with her outlook on life.

We must not lose hope ever. People do rise and grant us a ray of hope sometimes. It can promise to become a beacon of light that will illuminate the pathway that leads to a brighter future in a world shrouded in the dark mist of hopelessness. These people are a breath of fresh air. Martin Luther King Jr.; former presidents George Washington and Abraham Lincoln, Albert Einstein, Nelson Mandela, and Malala Yousafzai, the youngest ever Nobel Prize laureate, are some of the prime examples that spring to mind. Then one day these champions depart. With time hope also thins. Of course, their causes do remain, even though times have changed.

But then there is this man of Nazareth who selflessly walked the much-trodden dusty streets of Jerusalem and crisscrossed the stormy Sea of Galilee, peddling a cause that to this day stands peerless. Having defied the cruelty of a Roman cross and death's deadly sting, He is still in the running. Of Him, Scripture says:

> Christ in you, the hope of glory.
>
> —*Colossians 1:27*

This is why we must not lose hope, ever.

Not Young, but Not Finished Either

The opening scriptural reference of this chapter took us back to the time of Joshua, the mighty man of valor who took on the reins of leading the children of Israel into the Promised Land when Moses, his mentor, died. He made this profound statement of raw passion a whopping forty-five years after Moses received the word of promise from God. It is noteworthy that Joshua maintains a raw passion for conquest and achievement, despite the countless battles he has fought. At eighty-five, he still has it in his heart to say:

> Now therefore, give me this mountain of which the LORD spoke in that day.
>
> —*Joshua 14:12*

Joshua shows us a thing or two about surviving. He probably didn't have very much going for him at eighty-five, but he certainly exhibited a raw passion for walking into the fullness of God's promises, even when they had taken a long time to come about. He was not fazed by the setbacks he encountered in fighting hostile tribes and no fewer than thirty-one assailant kings, including the kings of Jericho, Ai, Jerusalem, Hebron, Jarmuth, Lachish, Eglon, Geder, Debir, Hormah, Arad, Libnah, Adullam, Makkedah, and Bethel. He wasn't done without taking the mountain he had been promised.

NO MATTER HOW HARD LIFE GETS OR HOW BAD YOUR PAST MAY HAVE BEEN, THERE STILL REMAINS A FUTURE WORTH WAITING FOR.

These battles involved direct physical confrontation with the enemy using pretty rudimentary military weaponry. Unlike modern-day warfare that employs state-of-the-art technology such as drones and unmanned flying gizmos to remotely destroy a target at the click of a button, Joshua's battles required direct physical contact man-to-man and the use of spears, swords, and bows. Joshua had felt the heat of battle, and he knew the pain of killing.

I wonder how the modern people of faith measure up in terms of raw passion for unconquered territory, unrealized dreams, and yet-to-be-seen hopes, especially when they are beset by tough times. I wonder whether many have the faith, courage, and impunity to seek to possess something greater than their past achievements and move on to possess an entire mountain for the kingdom of God.

Granted, times have changed, and circumstances are different.

Inflation has got to be factored in, and global population growth is a reality. However, can we really dismiss the importance of our passion in our pursuit of more fulfilling and wholesome living? Should the capacity to grow into our destiny be sacrificed on the altar of a lack of passion?

When we find ourselves lagging behind on delivering on the assignments that rest on our lives, we must learn to treat age as just a number. Jack Canfield writes:

> *Passion is something within you that provides the continual enthusiasm, focus, and energy you need to succeed. But unlike feel-good motivation derived from external sources, true passion has a more spiritual nature. It comes from within. And it can be channeled into amazing feats of success.*[3]

Seven Passions We Need

The following passions are necessary. They include a passion for God, the Word, prayer, people, purpose, progress, and family. Everyone needs them. Let's look at each one.

1. A Passion for God

It is imperative that we develop a passion for God, especially if we expect to survive trials. King David expressed his passion for God thus:

> *Truly my soul silently waits for God; from Him comes my salvation.*
>
> *—Psalm 62:1*

While God is omnipresent, omniscient, and omnipotent, He remains hidden and veiled from those who won't proactively and intentionally seek Him. He is everywhere all the time, but His manifest presence and manifold power do not always directly translate into our reality, nor are they automatically experienced by everyone. He only reveals Himself to the people who carry within their hearts a burning passion for Him. When people have a passion for God, it will be seen in their pursuit of Him. In Hebrews we read this:

> *But without faith it is impossible to please Him, for he who comes to God must believe that He is, and that **He is a rewarder of those who diligently seek Him.***
>
> —*Hebrews 11:6, emphasis added*

2. A Passion for the Word

The importance of the Word of God cannot possibly be emphasized enough in these pages. Bearing a passion for God ought to be closely followed by a passion for His Word because the two are eternally inseparable. God is as good as His Word. For this reason alone, He always makes good on His promises in His Word. God's Word has the capacity to reveal our innermost thoughts and purposes and have a great impact on our lives.

Attitude of servanthood. The greatest example of a servant leader the world has ever seen is Jesus Christ. Driven by the perfect love He had for all of mankind, He was not only competent enough but totally committed to the redemption of humanity, freeing us from the grip of sin and its effects to the point of paying the ultimate price with His own blood. Options were open and available, but He willingly chose to do that, laying down all the glory, power, and majesty that He commanded in the process.

> Let this mind be in you which was also in Christ Jesus, who, being in the form of God, did not consider it robbery to be equal with God, **but made Himself** of no reputation, taking the form of a bondservant, **and** coming in the likeness of men. And being found in appearance as a man, **He humbled Himself** and became obedient to the point of death, even the death of the cross.
>
> —Philippians 2:5–8, emphasis added

Jesus deliberately stripped Himself of His own reputation. It is kind of hard to make yourself of no reputation, if you never had a good one in the first place. But Jesus had such a great reputation before He stooped down to become a human. This required a deliberate effort on His part to humble Himself so He could include all people in His redemption. He did this because He desired to model an attitude of servanthood to us.

Jesus's teachings were marked by an emphasis on servanthood, which He labored to instill in His disciples and followers. He said:

> But whoever desires to become great among you shall be your servant.
>
> —Mark 10:43

Altitude of strongholds. By definition, strongholds are deep issues that hold us. They firmly grip their victims. From the Word of God we learn that they are supposed to be pulled down. Anything that we must pull down must be wrongfully set where it does not belong in the first place. Strongholds are therefore in an exalted position illegitimately. They are not supposed to be there. The Bible says:

> For the weapons of our warfare are not carnal but mighty in God for pulling down strongholds, casting down arguments and every high thing that exalts itself against the knowledge of God.

> —2 Corinthians 10:4–5

From this we can see that a stronghold is a spiritual fortress made up of wrongful thoughts that gives the enemy an area of influence in a person's life. Strongholds function and exert their influence from a superior mental altitude. However, they can and must be pulled down using the spiritual weaponry that the person of faith in Christ already possesses.

Beatitude of sufferance. The Word of God clearly commends the virtue of endurance and prescribes it to each and every person. Paul certainly recommended it to Timothy when he wrote, "You therefore must endure hardship as a good soldier of Jesus Christ" (2 Tim. 2:3). Endurance is related to sufferance, which is defined as the capacity to endure pain or hardship. There is something undeniably great about sufferance. We live in a pain-ridden world, and we have much need of endurance to get through it. Speaking of Christ, the writer of Hebrews shows us that something beautiful can come out of sufferance when he says:

> Though He was a Son, yet He learned obedience by the things which He suffered.

> –Hebrews 5 :8

Certitude of sanctification. The Word of God quite ably frees us from any doubts whatsoever about our sanctification once we come home to God through Christ and remain in union with Him in a posture of contrition. Sanctification is the progressive process by which the believer is set free from the power of sin. Certitude is defined as freedom from doubt, especially in matters of faith. It is certainty. Scripture says:

Therefore, if anyone is in Christ, he is a new creation; old things have passed away; behold, all things have become new.

–2 Corinthians 5 :17

Stand fast therefore in the liberty by which Christ has made us free, and do not be entangled again with a yoke of bondage.

–Galatians 5 :1

Exactitude of Scripture. The Word of God is precise, piercing, and purging. It is timeless and utterly relevant. It has stood the test of time and withstood the fiercest storms beating against it and yet has remained as exact as it has always been. From the writer of Hebrews, we learn this:

For the word of God is living and active and full of power [making it operative, energizing, and effective]. It is sharper than any two-edged sword, penetrating as far as the division of the soul and spirit [the completeness of a person], and of both joints and marrow [the deepest parts of our nature], exposing and judging the very thoughts and intentions of the heart.[1]

—Hebrews 4:12, AMP

Fortitude of sonship. The curse of modern-day living is

fatherlessness. We do not yet know what the far-reaching effects of fatherlessness will be, but increasingly women all over the world are having to be both mother and father to their children. Unfortunately, being a mother is already a tall order. The result is that fewer young men are developing with a good sense of direction since they have not learned it from their own fathers. These young men are the fathers of tomorrow.

In the African-American community alone, for example, more than 70 percent of children are born and raised out of wedlock by a single parent.[5] The fathers are absent. Further studies show that the shortage of male role models is like an express train headed straight for prison.

In September 2017, economist Dr. Walter E. Williams was quoted as saying:

> The No. 1 problem among blacks is the effects stemming from a very weak family structure. Children from fatherless homes are likelier to drop out of high school, die by suicide, have behavioral disorders, join gangs, commit crimes and end up in prison.[6]

The Word of God is the real benefit. It is a beacon of light that promises to light up the future by laying bare the strength in sonship and making it accessible to all. The Bible says:

> But as many as received him, to them gave he power to become the sons of God, even to them that believe on his name.
>
> —John 1:12, KJV

Magnitude of salvation. Salvation is a *big* deal. The salvation of mankind from the grip of sin and its deadly effects is the major concern of the entire Bible. Salvation is the love of God poured out for mankind. The Word of God takes great pains to reveal the magnitude of salvation. The good news is that at the close of the book, we win! We may take a licking in the interim, but at the end of the day, we cross the finish line in strength and power as the undisputed champions in a league of our own.

> *And hope maketh not ashamed; because the love of God is shed abroad in our hearts by the Holy Ghost which is given unto us.*
>
> *—Romans 5:5, KJV*

Rectitude of saintliness. Even though we live in a fallen world where evil is glorified, virtues are vilified, and sin is justified, righteousness remains a practical and relevant ideal. It may look old-fashioned to live a holy life, but right living will protect us. Evil will never replace good. The Bible teaches us this:

> *Righteousness exalts a nation, but sin is a reproach to any people.*
>
> *—Proverbs 14:34*

Servitude of sin. The showdown between mankind and sin runs as a single thread throughout the entire Bible. Whereas man is incapable of single-handedly fending off and conquering sin without divine assistance, God constantly rescues man through His varied messengers, both angelic and human. Sin is a cruel taskmaster, which leads to death in the end. Sin first fascinates you then assassinates you. Service to the whims of sin certainly never leaves anyone scorch-free but makes us all slaves instead.

> *For the wages of sin is death, but the gift of God is eternal life in Christ Jesus our Lord.*
>
> *—Romans 6:23*

Solitude of success. It can be lonely at the top. The quest for success always demands that we master living in solitude *without being lonely*. We cannot expect success if we choose to live and behave like everybody else. Greatness is often bred and nurtured in quiet, but sometimes that is what it takes to reach our dreams. The good news is that solitude and loneliness are not synonymous. You can be alone without being lonely. In the Word of God, we find a pretty interesting practice that demonstrates that solitude was a great secret to Jesus' success. It says:

> *Now in the morning, having risen a long while before daylight, He went out and departed to a solitary place; and there He prayed.*
>
> *– Mark 1 :35*

3. A Passion for Prayer

Prayer is a potent lifeline amid the throes of a trial. Unfortunately, many people resort to prayer only when all else has failed. They look at prayer as they do calling emergency services. That's too late. Napoleon Hill wrote (emphasis added):

> *If you are an observing person, you must have noticed that most people resort to prayer only after everything else has*

failed! Or else they pray by a ritual of meaningless words. And, because it is a fact that most people who pray do so only after everything else has failed, they go to prayer with their minds filled with fear and doubt, which are the emotions the subconscious mind acts upon, and passes on to Infinite Intelligence. Likewise, that is the emotion which Infinite Intelligence receives, and acts upon.[7]

The only antidote to this is to engage in prayer all the time— every day speaking to God, listening to His voice, and walking in healthy relationship with Him as a friend would.

GREATNESS IS OFTEN BRED AND NURTURED IN A QUIET PLACE.

---

4. A Passion for People

We must have passion for others. Insensitive people make dealing with trials worse, but godly friends are indispensable in this instance for two reasons. First, people are the resources that God has chosen to bring aid and encouragement to our lives. Secondly, we were intentionally created to be social creatures whose destiny and survival hinge on the health of our relationships.

5. A Passion for Purpose

Purpose is the clearly defined sense of direction that we all ought to possess. After twenty-two years of research into the wealthiest people in America, Napoleon Hill once wrote that all great success began with a "definite major purpose."[8]

Purpose gives meaning to life. Soldiering on without any sense of direction is a recipe for disaster. No one wants to be a wanderer his whole life long. We want to be filled with real purpose. We must, therefore, desire and find that purpose. Real happiness is a by-product of purpose, so the underlying guarantee for happiness is having purpose, knowing what we are to accomplish with our time here. This brings fulfillment to our lives.

6. A Passion for Progress

Those of us with a passion for progress have our hearts in the right place. Today our survival depends on information, knowledge, and wisdom. We will not make much progress if we are not hungry to learn more than we already know. That being said, it is worth noting that although God places no premium on ignorance, a lofty and puffed-up intellect that is not submissive to the Spirit of God is prone to pride and rebellion and will not prosper in the things of God.

7. A Passion for Family

The family unit is the basic building block upon which society and also the church are built. To neglect the family is to neglect the nation. To uphold and promote the family is to uphold and promote the nation. When God instituted the first family in the beginning, He demonstrated in practical terms that the family unit had a special place in His heart. Therefore, when we care for our families, we agree with God's plan. Mankind was created in the image and likeness of a Creator and established as a family unit from the beginning. That's significant. Since that time, the family has been satan's primary target in his diabolical agenda. This only underscores the uniqueness of family. The devil never goes after anything of no value. He is not stupid, only sly. On our end, dedication to our own families and an eye for encouraging those around us is hugely important for the health of God's kingdom.

CHAPTER 12

REGIMENTED PLANTING

Isaac planted crops in that land and took in a huge harvest. God blessed him. The man got richer and richer by the day until he was very wealthy. He accumulated flocks and herds and many, many servants, so much so that the Philistines began to envy him.

—Genesis 26:12–14, MSG

When man was created, he was endowed with immense potential and equipped with incredible mental abilities. His intellectual faculties made him capable of reason, analysis, innovation, and creativity, which he first showcased in the naming of all the animals, the management of the garden, and the skillful work of his hands. He started his earthly odyssey in a prepared setting bestowed with natural resources as a deliberate choice on the part of his Creator.

Adam and Eve were not perfect. They were just innocent but carried a natural propensity to sin lying dormant within them. Their imperfection meant that there was work to do. Responsible living was expected if they were to realize their full potential. They were a work in progress. They were to develop on the inside and allow that to manifest on the outside, not the other way around.

This should paint a compelling picture of the systems and structures that were put in place by God for the benefit and prosperity of mankind. One of the systems was that of seedtime and harvest. We read this in the Bible:

> *While the earth remains, seedtime and harvest, cold and heat, winter and summer, and day and night shall not cease.*
>
> *—Genesis 8:22*

Divine Order

There is a consistency that God built into His economic system of increase from the outset, which many people seem to fail to come into sync with so as to reap the harvest they desire. Anyone desiring to successfully break through to a prosperous and blessed life must have a consistent divine order so their desired goal can be achieved. Let's break this down.

Note that God did *not* say while the earth remains, harvest and seedtime, and so on. He actually said, "While the earth remains, seedtime and harvest." The planting precedes the plucking. God's divine order of increase will be short-circuited if we seek to harvest first before we've sown. This seems to be the reason why many people are deprived of the blessings they desire. We must engage in regimented planting, even when times are hard.

In the opening scriptural reference of this chapter, this consistent behavior is underscored again. Isaac was dovetailing his famine-survival paradigm with divine order when he "planted crops in that land and took in a huge harvest."

Would Isaac have seen the blessings that he did had he taken in a huge harvest first and then planted later? Of course not. There was famine in the land, so there was no harvest to reap. Resources were scanty, and most people had deserted the place and fled to Egypt in search of greener pastures. But Isaac was to learn that there could be increase in the middle of poverty. As Sam Wilkin writes, "The worst place to do business is really the best."[1]

Centuries after Isaac survived the famine by following divine order, King Solomon wrote this:

In the morning sow your seed, and in the evening do not withhold your hand; for you do not know which will prosper, either this or that, or whether both alike will be good.

—Ecclesiastes 11:6

Once again, the prosperity and the good in this verse are preceded by sowing—both in the morning and in the evening. This is regimented planting.

THERE CAN BE INCREASE RIGHT IN THE MIDDLE OF POVERTY.

Rich, Richer, Wealthy

The opening scriptural reference to this chapter presented three levels of affluence that God wants us to experience. They are rich, richer, and wealthy, very wealthy. God's design is that we should grow rich and keep getting richer until we are very wealthy. Just rich is not good enough. God wants to give us wealth.

The only reason Isaac sped through these levels of affluence during a famine was that he proactively participated in regimented planting.

Note the sequence of events. Page back and read that passage again.

God blessed the work of Isaac's hands, not the wishes of his heart. With that in mind, do you think you have a part to play in your own deliverance? Absolutely! When you are in dire straits and in the throes of a dreadful experience, there are still many ways God can rescue you, provided you do your part. You must do the planting, the irrigation, the weeding, and the waiting. Your hands might be blistered, but God's hand will bring blessings.

IT IS NOT GOOD ENOUGH TO SIMPLY BECOME RICH.

Seeds and Needs—the Showdown

Seed is the custodian of bounty. Just as a woman goes into labor at full term to deliver the seed that was implanted in her body, we have to labor to bring forth the increase deposited in the wombs of our minds.

The mind is the incubator of thought, ideas, aspirations, dreams, visions, and purpose. All these are the seed that eventually develops into success, well-being, happiness, prosperity, and fulfillment. Your proactive and mandatory cooperation in this equation is the means by which the seed is translated from the cocoon of potential into the continuous network of plenty.

The seed you plant today is the answer to the need you'll encounter tomorrow. To flout the seed is to forfeit the harvest. When you stray with the seed, you stay with the need. When we are steadfast in the planting, seed grows. Jesus taught this.

Unless a grain of wheat falls into the ground and dies, it remains alone; but if it dies, it produces much grain.

—John 12:24

The picture Jesus presented holds true in both the literal and allegorical sense. Literally, a seed goes into the ground, breaks open (or dies), and sends a new shoot upward to produce a new plant after its kind. Jesus actually fell into the ground after His death. On the third day, He resurrected in fulfillment of an agelong prophecy in the garden of Eden. (See Gen. 3:15.) Henceforth, His disciples and followers began to multiply, and the ripple effect still continues as souls turn to God by the hundreds of thousands each day. That "grain of wheat" is continually producing more after its own kind.

This is the exact process by which increase comes about in the natural realm. Through this process, Isaac gained a bumper crop that sparked his progression from rich through richer to wealthy.

Agrarian Antics

We live in a drive-through breakthrough-crazed generation marked by temperamental relational loyalty. It is commonplace to drive to a fast-food restaurant, place your order in one minute, and drive away with your meal in the next. When one chain falters in this craze, disloyalty promptly rears its ugly head as the previously faithful nonchalantly switch their loyalty to another. When you get home from a long day's work, you place your frozen dinner in a microwave and retrieve it minutes later, and you're good to go. People can now opt for drive-through weddings. Some even expect some type of drive-through sermon in church. A fiery guest preacher at a certain church once asked how much time he had to get through his sermon. Nothing could have prepared him for the answer he got. He was told that after fifteen minutes he was at liberty to keep firing away *at the empty pews* to his satisfaction, but he should make sure all the doors and windows were properly locked and the keys returned to the caretaker (comfortably watching his favorite football team in a televised playoff nearby) when he was done!

Ours is also a survival-of-the-technically-savvy era. New technologies ignite worldwide furor. They are developing so fast that by the time graduates of IT degree programs walk across the stage, much of what they've been learning is already obsolete. I sometimes feel like a dinosaur, although my nostalgia does not get much sympathy from the millennials who currently rule the world.

Our fast-food, microwave, instant gratification, convenience-driven, postmodern culture adversely conditions us, putting us at odds with the agriculturally minded God we seek to know better. This is one major reason people in tough times struggle to understand why their frantic pleas for a quick fix seem to fall on deaf ears. Chagrined by this seeming indifference toward their pain on the part of their Creator, they give in to distress and despair. They find His 'slow' response to their plight overwhelming, as if their own speedy, but futile, reaction was any better. Tossed between pillar and post, they often throw in the towel or hang up their gloves. The angrier ones do both.

Eyes welling up with tears

While demons chortle and cheer;

Fate and chance, their agitated outbursts hear

Yet still usurp the reins; as their destiny to the gallows steers.

But God is, and has always been, agricultural. He thinks and works in agrarian ways, and to qualify this, you only need to look at the beginning.

*The LORD God **planted a garden** eastward in Eden. . . . And **out of the ground** the LORD God made every tree grow that is pleasant to the sight and good for food.*

—Genesis 2:8–9, emphasis added

Can you imagine an all-powerful, all-knowing Creator wearing His work gear and reaching for His farming implements just after

He spoke all of creation into existence? Evidently this job was considered pleasant and good. Although He was capable of starting the entire ecosystem from its most mature state onward, He opted for the long and arduous process of organically developing it from the ground up instead.

But this agrarian feat was only in line with what had been done already. A precedent had been set. The man for whom the garden was being planted was himself a by-product of this mind-set—the agricultural paradigm that informed God's workmanship.

This is the history of the heavens and the earth when they were created, in the day that the Lord *God made the earth and the heavens, before any plant of the field was in the earth and before any herb of the field had grown. For the* Lord *God had not caused it to rain on the earth, and there was **no man to till the ground**; but a mist went up from the earth and watered the whole face of the ground. And the* Lord *God **formed man of the dust of the ground**, and breathed into his nostrils the breath of life; and man became a living being.*

—*Genesis 2:4–7, emphasis added*

To this day, not much has changed regarding God's agricultural mind-set. He insists on this focus, and it doesn't look as if He's about to change that anytime soon. In fact, He declared:

For I am the Lord, *I do not change.*

—*Malachi 3:6*

The next time you ask Him to meet your need, be sure that He'll draw your attention to your seed. Why? Because within the nooks and crannies of every seed resides the harvest that you seek. From the very beginning, He set things up to function around the seed system.

> And God said, "See, I have given you every herb that yields **seed** which is on the face of all the earth, and every tree whose fruit yields **seed**; to you it shall be for food."
>
> —Genesis 1:29, emphasis added

God is into organic solutions. Organic produce requires natural conditions in order to thrive and bear organic fruit. It also requires time, lots of it—seasons of rain and seasons of sunshine, as well as seedtime and harvest, weeding, pruning, purging, watering, and waiting. All of these words spring to mind. People who are out of that loop hate these words.

WHEN YOU STRAY ON THE SEED, YOU STAY WITH THE NEED.

The genetic modification of foods is a tale of someone trying to go down unorthodox routes to cut corners but still get bigger, brighter, and more bountiful dividends. Genetic modification tweaks the DNA using genetic engineering to introduce new traits into organisms that allow us to control the final results.

Residual Potential in What Is Left

While on holiday in Uganda in the summer of 2017, I read an article published in *New Vision*, the country's flagship daily, that catapulted me from disgust to delight in quick succession. It was the story of a secondary school in the suburbs of the country's eastern town of Tororo that was proudly talking about excrement. Don't turn away yet; that is not the end of the story. The article chronicled the ingenious procedure of processing and profiting from the sewage and fecal waste of the school's latrines. By generating bioenergy from something worthless and converting it into something worthwhile, this school blazed a trail that ought to be emulated globally. The ingenuity of turning something disgusting into a benefit touched and blessed my soul.

IF ANYTHING IS TO QUALIFY AS PLEASANT AND GOOD, IT MUST BE GROWN.

Nasty can turn into nice. In the aftermath of a raging storm, we can always salvage something. This is not always obvious, but it is there nevertheless. When the dust settles, something remains. When disaster strikes, a legacy emerges. In the end, we treat the disaster as a close call, no matter what is left behind. Whether what is left retains its original sheen is not the issue. We focus on tapping into the remaining potential instead.

The greatest challenge, however, is finding that remaining

seed from which new life can be formed so that we can make a comeback. This can be a difficult task, but the Bible says:

> *"For there is hope for a tree, if it is cut down, that it will sprout again, and that its tender shoots will not cease. Though its root may grow old in the earth, and its stump may die in the ground,* **yet at the scent of water it will bud and bring forth branches like a plant.**
>
> *—Job 14:7–9, emphasis added*

The article about Uganda pointed out that there was potential and purpose in what was left. Let's dig into the two ideas of potential and purpose.

WITHIN THE NOOKS AND CRANNIES OF EVERY SEED RESIDES THE HARVEST THAT YOU SEEK.

Potential

One interesting definition of *potential* is "a latent excellence or ability that may or may not be developed."[3] Obviously, whether "excellence or ability" is actually developed is another subject, but for now the point stands that potential is *latent* ability. It is hidden. It stands to reason, then, that in the wake of trouble, any residual energy ought to be spent nursing back to life whatever is left instead of sullenly licking the wounds of what was lost. Looking for what remains has potential; pouting doesn't.

Our miracle is never in what we lost but always in what we have left. Our success is not found in our ability to elude trouble and play it safe but in the art and craft of sewing the shreds that trouble left behind into a useful garment. The miracle is in the ability to hang in there while an important relationship suffers because of stubborn egos. This is priceless! Our survival rests on our ability to glue the shattered pieces of a broken dream back together.

One of the biggest problems with unsuccessful people is their inability to see pain as a great motivational force. As a result, they live resigned and settle for a life of regret—bitterly recounting what should have been.

Purpose

We've discussed purpose in an earlier chapter, but I'd like to add this thought: If you thought long and deep about what remains after a trial, you would only come to the single conclusion that what is left is there for a purpose. God never creates purposeless things. The enemy only attacks purpose.

OUR MIRACLE IS NEVER IN WHAT WE LOST BUT ALWAYS IN WHAT WE HAVE LEFT.

Eight Truths about Seed

We don't have to buck the system and leave our survival to chance, stoically hoping for a lucky break, to get out of a trial. These eight truths can give us a clear and focused perspective on seeds and their growth.

1. **The responsibility of seed planting rests solely on us.** If you remember, Isaac did the planting, and God did the blessing. This underscores the importance of doing your part in all things faith related and letting God do His part. God's blessing can only be bestowed on the work of your hands. Blessings do not fall on people's laps like ripe bananas. The days of manna falling out of the blue are long gone.

2. **The domain where you plant your seed is the domain where you reap your harvest.** It is hard to reap from where you did not sow. The Bible is very clear on this point.

   For he who sows to his flesh will of the flesh reap corruption, but he who sows to the Spirit will of the Spirit reap everlasting life.

   —*Galatians 6:8*

3. **Seed planting is nobler than crop harvesting.** Maturity demands that you outgrow celebrating only the harvest. It requires that you celebrate the planting of the seed too because there will be no gathering where there has been no planting. Seed planting is the father of crop harvesting. In other words, giving is greater than receiving. All shortage can be traced to stinginess.

   Remember the words of the Lord Jesus, that He said, "It is more blessed to give than to receive."

—Acts 20:35

4. **The quality of the seed you plant determines the quality of the harvest you reap.** I was raised to observe the practically religious custom of retreating to the countryside for every school holiday. Once in our rural setting where my dad reared farm animals and farmed, we were to learn the process of maintaining a good breed of cattle in our herds from firsthand experience.

My father often brought thoroughbred bulls, bought or borrowed, to cross with his cows to produce the desired hybrid calves. They were specially bred to withstand adverse conditions and the many ailments that peppered the savanna, thanks to the more resilient and robust pedigree they stemmed from. My father knew that the quality of the calves he was rearing was a function of the quality of the thoroughbreds from which they were descended.

5. **The quantity of the seed you plant determines the quantity of the crop you harvest.** When it comes to seed planting, numbers matter. There is a strong correlation between the amount planted and the amount reaped.

   For with the same measure that you use, it will be measured back to you.

   —Luke 6:38

When well-meaning folks go about sulking over the meager results they are achieving in their lives, they're bound to put the blame on God, saying, "God planned this miserable harvest!" The Bible does not agree with that. God doesn't determine the harvest you reap. The quantity of the seed *you plant* does.

He who sows sparingly will also reap sparingly, and he who sows bountifully will also reap bountifully.

—2 Corinthians 9:6

6. **The nature of the seed planted determines the nature of the harvest.** What you reap in life reflects the seed you sowed. The peculiar characteristics and idiosyncrasies of the end result you experience are a clone of those within the seed from which they sprang. If you don't like the harvest you are reaping and need to rectify it, the culprit to address is the seed. Paul taught this:

Whatever a man sows, that he will also reap.

—Galatians 6:7

Seed reproduces after its own kind (Gen. 1:12). You go ahead and keep sowing goodwill toward others, and sooner than later, goodwill will become the staple of your story. You go ahead and keep sowing financial seed into the lives of others, and you will reap a financial harvest as a consequence. You keep sowing items of clothing into the good ground of other people's lives, and you will see your own wardrobe bursting at the seams.

On the flip side, if you sow discord among others (Prov. 6:14, 19), you will taste of your own medicine as turmoil and chaos show up at your doorstep, and it will also be in good measure, pressed down, shaken together, and running over! Jesus illustrated it deeper when He taught that:

For a good tree does not bear bad fruit, nor does a bad tree bear good fruit. For every tree is known by its own fruit. For men do not gather figs from thorns, nor do they gather grapes from a bramble bush.

—Luke 6:43–44

7. **The soil matters.** Different regions of the world are ideal for the growth and fruitfulness of different plant species. It is with good reason that tropical vegetation does not thrive in temperate lands. Likewise, many plants that would do well in temperate conditions would struggle to survive, let alone thrive, in tropical conditions. It matters where you plant your seed.

When Jesus taught the parable of the sower, as recorded in Mark 4:1–8, He unveiled the four kinds of grounds into which seed could be sown: the path, the stony ground, the thorny ground, and the good ground. As it happens, these are also the four kinds of hearts people have. Jesus taught that only the good ground guaranteed a bumper crop at harvesttime.

8. **Seed growing takes time.** My wife tells the story of her first experience planting bean seeds in her home garden as a child. She was seething with excitement the morning after she planted those beans, scouring through the soil to find the plants. In the process, she unearthed the seeds to see their progress. She found they had hardly changed despite her heartfelt and hands-on labor the day before. Upset, she sought out her aunt, demanding an explanation. Her aunt replied simply, "Seed growing doesn't work like that."

Seed growth requires time and patience on our part. It will be a long time before the plant grows and bears fruit. Joyce Meyer is quoted as once saying, "Patience is not simply the ability to wait—it's how we behave while we're waiting."[4]

One cannot help but wonder whether many remain that will have the patience and character to let the seeds they've planted in the gardens of their lives grow without needlessly interrupting that growth, as my wife did as a child. We must patiently wait.

*See how the farmer waits for the precious fruit of the earth, waiting patiently for it until it receives the early and latter rain. **You also be patient. Establish your hearts.***

—*James 5:7–8, emphasis added*

EPILOGUE

We can survive tough times, and miracles do happen. And I do mean real miracles, even in this postmodern and high-tech era in which social media and political correctness are all the rage and civil liberties are a hot potato. No one would share a message on surviving and pulling through hardship if there wasn't sufficient experiential testimony and scriptural evidence to support it. And there is. I could not here recount all the ways God has rescued and grown His children, but He has. This message is bona fide, with a broad-ranging variety of witnesses who could attest to its validity.

However, way too many still subscribe to the belief that miracles are only the holy grail of deep religiosity and a staple of the paranormal world, which these folks have little control over. These people need to be won over to the reality that miracles are the phenomena that happen when ordinary people partake in the process God planned from the beginning. Miracles happen when we partner with God. As we do that, deliverance and success are achieved in time. We can survive tough times best when we discern and cooperate with the positive undercurrents that work to ensure our victory.

There is something to take from Michael Jordan's words. The retired professional basketball player once said: "Some people want it to happen, some wish it would happen, others make it happen."[1]

Enroll at the "others" club. Make it happen. You will survive anything that threatens your life. As you do, you will be cheered to the rafters by God, His angels, and the people in your life that count.

When John the revelator was asked by one of the elders in Revelation 7 to identify the people he had seen in his vision arrayed in white robes, he answered, "Sir, you know." Then the elder said:

> These are the ones who come out of the great tribulation, and washed their robes and made them white in the blood of the Lamb.
>
> —Revelation 7:14

Upon the authority of the Word of God, I say to you, come out of your tribulation and survive!

END NOTES

Introduction

1 Daren A. Benzi, *Motivated or Misplaced?* (n.p., 2018), foreword by Les Brown, https://www.amazon.com/Motivated-Misplaced-Steps-Create-Life/dp/1717817408/ref=sr_1_1?keywords=Motivated+or+Misplaced%3F&qid=1575907894&sr=8-1.

Chapter 1

1 Edward M. Bounds, *Guide to Spiritual Warfare* (New Kensington, PA: Whitaker House, 1984), 103.

2 Colleen McDannell, *Religions of the United States in Practice*, vol. 2 (Princeton, NJ: Princeton University Press, 2001).

3 Dr. Myles Munroe, *Understanding the Purpose and Power of Prayer* (New Kensington, PA: Whitaker House, 2003), 151.

4 Jack Canfield with Janet Switzer, *The Success Principles: How to Get from Where You Are to Where You Want to Be* (New York: HarperCollins Publishers, 2005).

5 Norman Vincent Peale, *The Power of Positive Thinking* (Plano, TX: Samaira Book Publishers, 2019).

Chapter 2

1 Albert Einstein, "Psychology Sayings and Quotes," Wise Old Sayings, accessed September 17, 2019, http://www.wiseoldsayings.com/psychology-quotes/.

2 *The American Heritage Dictionary of the English Language*, s.v. "resilient," accessed December 9, 2019, https://tinyurl.com/rvmyu6y.

3 Brian Tracy and Christina Tracy Stein, *Kiss That Frog! 12 Great Ways to Turn Negatives into Positives in Your Life and Work* (San Francisco, CA: Berrett-Koehler Publishers, 2012), 78.

4 "Raymond Holliwell Quotes," Quotes.net, accessed December 10, 2019, https://www.quotes.net/quote/43074.

5 Sheryl Estrada, "Denzel Washington at NAACP Image Awards: 'Ease Is a

Greater Threat to Progress than Hardship,'" DiversityInc, February 14, 2017, https://www.diversityinc.com/denzel-washington-naacp-image-awards-ease-greater-threat-progress-hardship/.

6 John MacArthur, *First Love* (Wheaton, IL: Victor Books, 1995), 59–60.

7 Victor E. Frankl, *Man's Search for Meaning* (New York: Pocket Books, 1959), 137.

8 Sharon Salzberg, *Faith: Trusting Your Own Deepest Experience* (New York: Penguin Putnam, 2002).

9 Rhonda Byrne, *The Secret* (New York: Atria Books, 2018), 109–110.

10 Les Brown, "Les Brown Quotes," BrainyQuote, accessed December 10, 2019, https://www.brainyquote.com/quotes/les_brown_389885.

Chapter 3

1 Graham Powell and Shirley Powell, *Christian, Set Yourself Free* (West Sussex: New Wine Press, 1983).

Chapter 4

1 "Sylvester Stallone Motivational Video," Motivation Mentalist, January 1, 2018, https://motivationmentalist.com/2018/01/01/sylvester-stallone-motivational-video/).

Chapter 5

1 Ryan Holiday, *The Obstacle Is the Way: The Timeless Art of Turning Trials into Triumph* (New York: Portfolio/Penguin, 2014), 112–113.

2 Alex W. Ness, *Holiness* (Pefferlaw, Ontario: Agape Publications, 1985), 213.

3 "Plato Quotes," Goodreads, accessed December 10, 2019, https://www.goodreads.com/quotes/263728-courage-is-knowing-what-not-to-fear.

4 Edward Mote and William Batchelder Bradbury, "My Hope Is Built on Nothing Less," hymnal.net, accessed December 10, 2019, https://www.hymnal.net/en/hymn/h/298.

Chapter 6

1 Max Lucado, *Six Hours One Friday: Anchoring to the Power of the Cross*

(Portland, OR: Multnomah, 1989), 87.

Chapter 7

1 Neil Thompson, *People Skills: 2nd ed.* (Hampshire: Palgrave Macmillan, 2002), 71.

2 "Thomas Paine Quotes," BrainyQuote, accessed December 10, 2019, https://www.brainyquote.com/quotes/thomas_paine_117868.

3 "Saint Augustine Quotes," BrainyQuote, accessed December 10, 2019, https://www.brainyquote.com/quotes/saint_augustine_148548.

4 "Aristotle Quotes," Goodreads, accessed December 10, 2019, https://www.goodreads.com/quotes/16892-patience-is-bitter-but-its-fruit-is-sweet.

Chapter 8

1 "Talent Wins Games, but Teamwork . . . Wins Championships," Leadership (blog), PennState, March 19, 2017, https://sites.psu.edu/leadership/2017/03/19/talent-wins-games-but-teamwork-wins-championships/.

2 Mike Williams, *The Road to Your Best Stuff* (Mike Williams Solutions, 2008), 28.

Williams, *The Road to Your Best Stuff*, 46.

4 *God's Little Devotional Book II* (Tulsa, OK: Honor Books, 1997), 47.

5 "Helen Keller," Wikipedia, updated December 14, 2019, https://en.wikipedia.org/wiki/Helen_Keller.

6 "Helen Keller," Wikipedia.

7 Helen Selsdon, "Helen Keller's Presidential Medal of Freedom," American Foundation for the Blind, June 12, 2014, https://www.afb.org/blog/entry/helen-kellers-presidential-medal-freedom.

8 "Helen Keller," Wikipedia.

9 "Helen Keller," Wikipedia.

Chapter 9

1 Brian Tracy, *Master Your Time, Master Your Life: The Breakthrough System to Get More Results, Faster, in Every Area of Your Life* (New York: Penguin Books, 2017), 31.

2 Jane Alexander, *The Overload Solution: What to Do When Life Gets out of Control* (London: Piatkus, 2005), 214.

3 Dr. Rob Yeung, *Confidence: Transform the Way You Feel so You Can Achieve the Things You Want* (Harlow, England: Pearson, 2013), 117.

4 Asad Meah, "Understanding the Law of Attraction with Bob Proctor," Awaken the Greatness Within, accessed December 12, 2019, https://www.awaken-thegreatnesswithin.com/understanding-law-attraction-bob-proctor/.

Chapter 10

1 Dictionary.com, s.v. "throne," accessed December 20, 2019, https://www.dictionary.com/browse/throne.

2 Max Lucado, *Facing Your Giants: God Still Does the Impossible* (Nashville: Thomas Nelson, 2006), 150.

3 Lisa Fields, "The Healing Power of Gratitude," Reader's Digest, accessed December 20, 2019, https://www.readersdigest.co.uk/health/health-conditions/the-healing-power-of-gratitude.

4 Fields, "The Healing Power of Gratitude."

5 Max Lucado, *Six Hours One Friday*.

Chapter 11

1 Dictionary.com, s.v. "passion," accessed December 20, 2019, https://www.dictionary.com/browse/passion.

2 "The Passion of the Christ," RogerEbert.com, February 24, 2004, https://www.rogerebert.com/reviews/the-passion-of-the-christ-2004.

3 Pat Mesiti, *Wake Up and Dream* (Sydney: Pat Mesiti Ministries, 1994), 21–22.

4 Canfield with Switzer, *The Success Principles*, 268.

5 Walter E. Williams, "The Welfare State's Legacy," Creators Syndicate, September 20, 2017, https://www.creators.com/read/walter-williams/09/17/the-welfare-states-legacy.

6 Williams, "The Welfare State's Legacy."

7 Napoleon Hill, *Think and Grow Rich* (Radford, VA: Wilder, 2007), 160.

8 Hill, *Think and Grow Rich*.

Chapter 12

1 Sam Wilkin, *Wealth Secrets: How the Rich Got Rich* (New York: Back Bay Books; Little, Brown and Company, 2015).

2 Potential definition #6 which is a noun, http://dictionary.com/

3 Joyce Meyer, https://www.themindfulword.org/2015/patience-quotes

Epilogue

1 "Michael Jordan Quotes," BrainyQuote, accessed December 20, 2019, https://www.brainyquote.com/quotes/michael_jordan_167382.

IF YOU'RE A FAN OF THIS BOOK, WILL YOU HELP ME SPREAD THE WORD?

There are several ways you can help me get the word out about the message of this book…

- Post a 5-Star review on Amazon.

- Write about the book on your Facebook, Twitter, Instagram, LinkedIn, – any social media you regularly use!

- If you blog, consider referencing the book, or publishing an excerpt from the book with a link back to my website. You have my permission to do this as long as you provide proper credit and backlinks.

- Recommend the book to friends – word-of-mouth is still the most effective form of advertising.

- Purchase additional copies to give away as gifts.

The best way to connect with me is by email at
Survingtoughtimes101@yahoo.com

You can order these books from

amazon **BARNES&NOBLE**

or where ever you purchase your favorite books.